To Sue & Mark

Don't You Want Somebody to Love

Reflections on the San Francisco Sound

The Great Society

Also
★ featuring
Don Garrett or Dan Hicks

Opening Tuesday June 21

DESIGN: WILLIAM RE

Don't You Want Somebody to Love

Reflections on the San Francisco Sound

A 25th Anniversary
"Summer of Love"
Presentation

by Darby Slick

SLG BOOKS
BERKELEY–HONG KONG

First Published 1991 by
SLG BOOKS
P.O. Box 9465
Berkeley, CA 94709
Tel: (510) 841-5525
Fax: (510) 841-5537

Cover Design: Yuk Wah Lee
Editor: Claire Burch
Design and Typesetting: Sara Glaser and Mark Weiman
Regent Press, Berkeley, California
Color separations and printing by
Snow Lion Graphics
Berkeley/Hong Kong

Library of Congress Cataloging-in-Publication Data

Slick, Darby, 1944-
Don't you want somebody to love:reflections on the San Francisco sound/by Darby Slick.
p. cm.
ISBN 0-943389-07-7:$29.95.
ISBN 0-943389-08-9 (pbk.):$15.95
1. Rock music–California–San Francisco–History and criticism.
2. Rock musicians–California–San Francisco. I. Title.
ML3534.S57 1991 91-27899
781.66'09794'6109046–dc20 CIP MN

For my mother,
who engendered in me
a love for art, and my wife Carol,
who kept me alive and
made me glad that she did,
and Maestro Ali Akbar Khan,
who taught me ninety percent of
what I know about music,
and gave the tools to learn
the other ten percent.

Preface

When I set out to write about my experiences of twenty five years ago in San Francisco, I made one rule; I would rely on my own memory. I didn't want to propagate another's errors. I have stuck to this, and undoubtedly my story contains versions of events with which others may disagree. I have tried to tell the truth as I remember it. For any falsities I apologize, and fall back on the words of the immortal Elwood Blues, "It's not lies, it's just bullshit."

Contents

1

Hunter-Gatherers

Something new was happening, and some didn't understand. As I walked with Grace into the nightclub where our band was appearing, the manager eyed Grace's dirty miniskirt, and my old boots and holey sweater and said, "Jesus Christ, if you want to look like fucking bums, why don't you at least put patches all over your clothes so people will know you're doing it on purpose." Grace turned her face sideways towards me and lifted her brows without smiling as we walked on into the darkened club. The manager was fortunate that Grace was not drunk, or her reaction would have been considerably less subtle. I chuckled almost silently as I shook my head from side to side.

We walked to the musician's room, an ex-closet, and began smoking the joint Grace had brought out of her feedbag purse. We laughed and joked with each other to cover our nervousness.

"I like that new zit on your nose." she said.

"Why, thank you very much. I think the purple rays spreading from it's base are especially fetching. Where's Jerry?"

"He'll be along. He had something to do." she said, with a look on her face that I couldn't make out; something was up.

"You know, maybe the the doorman's right," I said, "that skirt looks like a dish-rag someone found all stiffened-up under a sink somewhere."

"Fuck you. Any way, you should talk, your sweater is so dirty its hard to tell where the moth holes are."

"God, this conversation is so witty. Here, finish it up." I said, handing Grace the roach. She took it in her long clear-covered nails, thumb and first finger, so that she could smoke it down to it's last little burst of flame without burning herself. She drank from a small bottle of the cheapest champagne; I drank beer. This was our homework, our preparation for the stage. Neither of us knew much about music, so we relied on "getting in the mood" to help us play well. Also, Grace knew how to grab men in the audience by the balls, but without alcohol, she lacked the courage to do so. For all our, "Fuck you, I don't care." attitude, we wanted to be liked.

And what was going on here that was new? It was the dance-drama transformation of the young beatniks into hippies. We had read the new poets: Allen Ginsberg, Lawrence Ferlinghetti; seen the new movies: Truffaut, Fellini; had heard the music of Miles and 'Trane and Stockhousen and John Cage and, most recently, the Stones and the Beatles. We were alive, for Christ's sake, and the fifties had to end. We would not even wear the funny suits of the Beatles, let them imitate us.

The other members of the band drifted in, my brother Jerry, Grace's husband, among them. He was carrying an unfamiliar case with him; it looked like a guitar case.

"Here." he said, handing it to me.

"What's that?"

"Open it up and see for yourself." There was no table or anything, so I sat down on a ratty old chair and opened the case on my lap. Inside was a new Guild guitar. It was red, had an almost hourglass shape, and in the back, there was a chrome bar you could pull out which would act as a stand to hold it up when you weren't playing it. I was very excited. When I started to play it, unamplified of course, I could feel that it played much more easily than my old one; I could hardly wait to hear how it sounded. Jerry had bought the guitar with the small bonus we had received for signing a record deal. I was thrilled to get it, but somewhere inside of me a voice was asking, "Shouldn't I have gotten to pick it out?"

It was time to play our first set of the night. By the end of the set, Grace would have sung lead on most of the songs and have played the guitar, bass, keyboard and the flute-like recorder. She and I would have traded solos back and forth,

"I hear you."

"I love you."

"I'll raise you one, or ten." spiralling, crashing, mood-warping, and then dropping back into the band music repeatedly. Many in the audience only wanted to look at her black-stockinged legs which, ironically, she regarded as her worst feature. The fucking platforms for the topless dancers were still in place, and half the audience were male business travelers wearing three piece suits who didn't know from anything about hippies. They had read about beatniks in Life Magazine, but they had no intention of going near any. It was just, "Bring on the girls."

We were playing here because the week before, Tom Donahue had signed our group, the Great Society, to a contract on his new record label. Our prize was to play at his new club, Mothers, for people who would have been happier with Trini Lopez.

I loved the feel of my new guitar, but had my doubts about its sound. I knew I'd have to give it some time and try various amp settings.

When the set was over, we went back to the dressing room. A beautiful young woman with shoulder-length golden hair walked in. She was wearing tight black short-shorts and a thin, white blouse, sort of closed with one button.

"Mind if I dance when you guys play again?" she asked, "I really like your music."

I looked at each person in the band, and they all made gestures of not caring, except David who shook his head up and down with a big grin, indicating unmitigated approval. "Sure," I said, "I don't know if it's cool with the club, but it's fine with us."

As I walked, stumbled, back towards the stage, I bumped into a table and knocked over a candle full of molten wax, spilling its contents on the coat and pants of one of the customers. Fear flooded over me, but he was only annoyed, not irate. When we began to play, the girl climbed onto a go-go platform, took off her blouse, and began to dance. Bizarre! I had never seen topless dancing; only squares went to topless clubs. She danced one of those specific dances, the Frug, I think, which allows little creativity. She must have been on a break from her topless job up the street, and was so into it, that she had come here to dance her break away. Her eyes were glassy. Perhaps she was hypnotized. She loved, or needed, the trance. We were playing music that was easy to dance to when suddenly, we went into a bridge in an odd rhythm. The dancer began to stumble. We were playing in seven/four, and each time she had one more beat, one more move, left to do in her pattern, we were already on the first beat of ours, and she would try to jump to the beginning instantaneously. She looked like she might lock her legs together and fall down at any moment. Though I thought her pretty, I took amused pleasure in her body-confusion. When the song was over, she left and didn't return.

Soon, at the Fillmore Auditorium and the Avalon Ballroom, people would invent freer ways to dance to the new music. Dancers would glide, swoop, spin, and careen, avoiding all of the steps shown on Dance Party and Shindig. But before we walk together through the psychedelic labyrinth that was San Francisco in the middle sixties, let's go back to the beginnings of the hippie era which were based on, or at least glued together by, the music scene.

What led to it all? How did we get there?

The main street of Palo Alto is lined with palm and fir trees. The houses along it are large and stately, and many have open porches, the roofs of which are supported by huge columns. The Importance of Being Stanford is everywhere. The nickname for the university is "the farm", and in the late forties and early fifties, the area was largely farms and orchards, plus, of course, the university, and the main street, which led directly over the railroad tracks, tracks which were so important in the university lore, to the university itself. The main street was named University Avenue.

The man Stanford was a railroad boss. The Golden Spike was the last spike driven into the Trans-Continental Railway, and it was housed at Stanford University; I know because I used to visit it regularly.

Every kid I knew went to every Stanford home football game. The shopping center was named the Stanford Shopping Center. The favorite burger place was named "S" Burger. The campus was the most popular destination for, first, our bike rides, and later, our make-out and drinking, car cruises. There were two movie theaters in town: the Varsity and the Stanford.

In the mid-forties, the area attracted many couples who were just starting families. Some of the men worked locally, most worked in "the city", and commuted on Stanford's train.

In the sixties, when the hippie thing started, it was really fueled by people who had been raised in the intellectual backyard of the university. Our educations in that climate must have been vastly more liberal than our parents'.

I'm going to name a few who came out of there, and though I'm going to miss many out of ignorance, I think the list will show the importance of that area to what followed. Dead: all. Quicksilver: David Freiburg. Big Brother: Peter Albin. Great Society: Jerry, Grace, me. Airplane: Jourma. Individuals: Joan Baez, Ken Kesey. We didn't all know each other, though many of us did; the point is, we were fired in the same furnace.

When I was still a Palo Alto baby, my mother hired a woman to help around the house. She lived a short block and a half away from us, and gradually, or maybe quickly, she became virtually a member of our family, and I of her's. Twenty five years later, my mother would die in her arms. Louise was a member of the local Baptist church, and her daughters often sang in the choir. When my parents went out of town, I used to stay with Louise and her family, and that meant going to church with them, and attending the choir rehearsals which often took place around the piano at their house. I remember people whispering and giggling about "the little white boy", but they were very loving towards me. Thus, I became immersed in Black gospel music at a formative age, and it is still profoundly important to me.

I learned to *play* my first music as a small child, under a flowering tree, on the beach at Waikiki, in the early fifties, when there were only a few hotels there. My teacher was an old Hawaiian named Dave. He taught Hawaiian music for the joy of it and received no money for his efforts. He was old and thin and was missing one of his front teeth. He always wore a faded captain's hat, dark slacks, and various Hawaiian shirts. He had a pair of thongs for the street, but went barefoot on the beach. He was not a virtuoso on the ukelele, but sang in that wonderful Hawaiian style of broad vibrato. He could also swing freely into falsetto voice for high parts (as in "the Hawaiian Wedding Song"). Three times a week, he would lead about thirty to forty people, almost all playing ukeleles, a few playing guitars, in an hour or so of music. Most of the participants were locals of various races; a few, like myself, were tourists. Many of the songs had little fill sections between the verses, which he would signal by shouting, "Cross the bar!" because the chord that began the fill was shaped like a bar. The air was sweet with the smell of flowers and tangy from the warm ocean. In the day time, we sat with our backs to the sun to protect our instruments. A tourist friend of mine who was about five years older than I was, Steve Mendel, helped me to learn some of the chords, and I practiced all day long when I got my first ukelele.

"I know it looks hard," said Steve, "but look. Here's a chord you can play with only one finger. You put your third finger on this first string, right past the second fret."

I tried, fumblingly, and said, "I'd rather use my first finger, okay?"

"Everyone wants to use their first finger. It's easier, but don't do it. When you learn a few more chords, you'll see why it's better to do it this way. Look, here's another one-finger chord. Put your second finger on the fourth string in the space after the first fret." I tried it and it was pretty easy. Within half an hour, I could rocket back and forth between these two, one-fingered chords, which I later learned are the heart of many fifties rock and roll songs.

By nightfall, I could play most of the simple chords on the ukelele. Every part of this experience was powerful for me: the music, the people, the sights and smells, the Hawaiian words of the songs, and the feeling of those strings under my fingers. We all put a little sand from the beach into the soundholes of our instruments for luck, and I would try throughout the years not to lose that sand.

Returning to Palo Alto, I hurried to my mother's closet, and having climbed through the hanging jungle of fragrant dresses, and over the flat boxes of moth-balled coats, I got out the slightly moldy old cardboard case that contained my grandfather's guitar. Next, I rode my thick-tired, one speed bike to the music store and bought a set of strings, and a Mel Bay instruction book with pictures dating from the twenties in it. I broke one of the strings trying to tune it up way too high (what did I know?) but soon had the guitar strung and tuned properly. I could see that the chord shapes for the first four strings were the same as those on the ukelele, so for the first two months I stuck with those, avoiding the two bass strings. I loved the sound of the metal guitar strings much more than I had the plastic ukelele strings, and the old guitar had great tone. Gradually, as my strength increased, I learned to play simple chords on all six strings. This guitar, which I thought the world of, was in some ways, not a very good one. The strings were too high off the fingerboard, and it took a lot of strength to push them down; my fingers got strong fast! Although I had many friends, I spent a lot of Saturdays alone with the guitar, and I practiced an hour or so every day. I learned many folk songs from records and books, and taught myself at least fake versions of various fingerpicking styles. Really, from that very first day in Hawaii, playing music was an irreplaceable part of my life; I valued it more than money.

While I was growing up, next door to me lived a fat little girl with buck teeth and a foul mouth named Grace Wing. She took piano lessons. She had friends, but when she was teased (which was often) she drove them away with the wrathful power of her mouth. She spent hours and days alone with her music and her dolls, living in magic worlds. She drew and painted. Her prodigious talents blossomed. My parents drank alcoholically; so, I think, did hers. When I was about eleven, I baby sat for her younger brother. The few moments that the now thin and cute, sixteen year old Grace spent with me after her date were hot stuff to me.

On the first day of junior high, I came to school wearing white bucks, white ducks, and a heliotrope and white, checked shirt. My blond hair was combed forward on the top, and back on the sides, in a d.a. I was getting into rhythm and blues and rock and roll. Little Richard was my favorite, and I still love his singing; he did quick, descending ornaments with his voice that really grabbed me. I also loved "Why do Fools Fall in Love", and

"Earth Angel" and many other hits of the day. When I heard "Little Darling", I had to have a drum set, and it had to have a cowbell so I could play that part from the record. My parents obliged me, and I began to practice drums as well as guitar. When I use the word "practice", don't let me fool you; I was having a ball playing along with records, and doing solos based on Gene Krupa's tom tom riff in "Sing Sing Sing".

Around this time, Ricky Nelson started singing on his family's t.v. show. My parents, seeing my interest in music, began to seriously consider finding me an agent who would try to turn me into a thirteen year old star. They decided, however, that it would be a bad life for me, so they didn't go ahead with it, and didn't mention it to me until I was about seventeen. Somehow, when I learned about how close I had come to at least trying for stardom, it really made me want to succeed in music; "I'll show you."

I continued playing drums and guitar through high school, sometimes playing snare drum in the school's marching band, but it was my older brother Jerry who really got into those pink and black drums. I was pretty good with the sticks, but he quickly got cooler at the interplay of the kick, snare and high-hat.

My younger brother Dan, began taking piano lessons. He started learning Scott Joplin songs, and listening to recorded versions of the same songs. This music, too, went into my little computer brain.

I think it was during my junior year that Grace and her family moved a few miles away. Grace went off to finishing school; she returned (finished), fell in love with my brother and they married. I thought they were the grooviest people on the face of the planet. To say I loved and admired them wouldn't be a strong enough statement.

After high school, in 1961, I went to college for one year.

It was August of 1962. Jerry, Grace, and I were at Jerryand my parents' beach house for the weekend. I had been asked not to return to the University of California at Santa Barbara for a semester or two because my grades had been so poor. I had cut far more classes than I had attended, and had filled in my schedule with drinking, dating, surfing and general carousing. The freshmen courses were less rigorous than my high school classes had been, and I could easily have excelled, but I couldn't be bothered. I had gone to a private high school, and later I learned that, while all of those who graduated with me had gone to college, within two years most had flunked out. It wasn't a lack of preparedness or intelligence; something was in the air.

I was at the beach house preparing myself to go into the army on Sunday evening; on Saturday night, I drank more than a case of beer. Sunday afternoon, Jerry and Grace drove me over to Fort Ord. Before they left me there, they gave me a little box of benzedrine pills. Grace looked me deep in the eyes as Jerry handed me the box. "It's only dope," she laughed, "maybe it'll help." As I watched them drive away, I felt like a prisoner, and indeed, I was.

A friend of mine, Lawrence, had been drafted about a month earlier, and he was at Fort Ord, so I decided to look him up. I found him lying on his bunk asleep. He was wearing a khaki uniform. I touched him on the shoulder, and he slowly rubbed the sleep out of his eyes. I think he had known that I was going into the army, but coming out of a sound afternoon sleep and finding me standing there was disorienting to him.

"What the fuck are you doing here?"

"Damned if I know."

"Oh Jesus, that's right, you joined up. I hate this fucking place." He was scratching his almost hairless head with the fingers of both hands.

"Thanks for the encouragement."

"I could lie."

"Naw, that's okay, but man, I'm gettin' cold feet."

"Well, you should have, but it's too late now."

It was great to see him, but soon I had to say goodby, and go find and join my own company. I didn't even consider sharing my new pills with him. They were the first dope I had ever had, other than booze and cigarettes, and they were precious to me.

When I arrived at my company, they started ordering me around, and they didn't stop, or even pause really, for twelve weeks. The highlights of my day would be when I would reach secretly into that little box and take a pill. I liked the effect and I liked having the secret. You think you're controlling my life, but I have a life you don't even know about.

Early in the morning, before sunrise, we would put on our heavy army clothes, including helmets, and go out for a long run. I could hear my heart pound, from the speed, before we even set out.

The days, and parts of the nights, were taken with exercise and training. I learned how to be a look-out, and how to take apart and assemble my rifle (*my* rifle!). I started avoiding segments of training when I could. It was often easy to leave the "going in" line and join the "coming out" one. I watched our sergeant play the old trick of making us hate him, and then love him, when we learned that he had done it all, all of the punishment, "for our own good." I saw through it, but felt the emotions anyway, and it pissed me off to be so consciously manipulated.

I was eighteen and the beat movement was still in full blossom. Word of it, which had drifted to me through newspaper articles and news reels, began to reach me more directly. I read several of the books that came out of the beatniks: *Howl, On The Road, A Coney Island of the Mind*, and others. With these works, the straight world which I had known, but had not completely loved, began to topple. These books did nothing to increase my love for military service, but I'm sure I would have hated it anyway. I had gone in, because the army had always seemed romantic to me, having encountered it as I had, only in books such as *The Naked and the Dead*. I know that Mailer didn't want to romanticize it, but for me he had. I was in for six months of active duty, and had a requirement of many years of monthly meetings and summer camps. During those initial six months, I decided that I was opposed to the military; reality had overtaken image, for me, and I just couldn't stand many aspects of military service, most importantly, my loss of personal freedom. Screaming, "Kill!" while charging a practice dummy with my bayonet, also turned me off, and forced me to face the reality of the situation. I don't know whether I would have had the strength of my convictions, but philosophically, I would rather have been killed than kill. I wrote a letter stating that I was a conscientious objector, and hand-delivered it to the company office where I was to sign up for summer camp. No one was at the office when I arrived, so I left my letter in the mail box. The old, one story building with it's fresh, thick paint covering decaying wood, had a deserted, forlorn look to which my single letter in the mailbox added. That was the last I heard from the army for seven years. The matter lay heavily on my mind the whole time, and I had frequent nightmares of having been reinducted. Later, a friend who had been a company clerk in the army, told me that he, and others, had routinely thrown people's files away; got a messy problem in the files and an inspection coming up? No sweat, just throw it away. This was one of the many blessings of that essentially pre-computer age. To place it in time, while I was serving my six months, our country invaded Cuba, and I received my travel pay and had my gear loaded onto boxcars; we were ready to cross the country and fight Castro. Though I did not want to fight, I had decided to go, because I couldn't imagine just running away.

When I got out of the army, I headed for North Beach, San Francisco's beat enclave. I left my army clothes to rot in a duffle bag, and resolved not to cut my hair for a long time.

North Beach had been settled largely by Italians, and they were in tune with many of the beat characteristics; they loved art, wine, music, leisurely mornings, afternoons, and evenings. I have no doubt they appeared to me happier than they really were, but they weren't as up-tight about long hair and quirky dispositions as were many Americans. It is hard to understand how threatening anything different was at that time. But here, it seemed that they had seen it all before, and it was not frightening to them.

North Beach was just as it should have been. On graceful hills and in alley ways, there were little coffee shops, bars, bookstores, jewelry shops, sandal shops, candle shops, art galleries, an old real pool hall, and many good cheap restaurants. Were the streets really cobbled, or does the "memory" just reflect how European it felt? If you were there at the time, the names return to you: City Lights, Mike's, the Spaghetti Factory, (fill in more). Often, on Sunday afternoons, Jerry, Grace and I used to go to North Beach to a little bar that featured Flamenco music. Local artists traded off with L.A.'s best, and sometimes players came from New York or even Spain. We, and the others, would sit around drinking cheap, red wine, and listening to the sometimes fiery, sometimes sad, music. Most Friday nights, we seemed to find a party given by a friend or a friend of a friend, and the crowds were wildly mixed; Forty Niners, stockbrokers, college kids, junkies, lawyers, we just threw ourselves together, it didn't matter with whom. On Saturday nights, we might go to listen to jazz, or poetry, or jazz and poetry combined. Usually, the jazz artists we heard were not very famous because we didn't always spend on the cover charge what we wanted to spend on drugs and alcohol. Often, we would do a lot of little things, and include a long stop at the bookstore; how many books had been written about Joyce's *Ulysses*? There seemed to be yards of them. "I'll take two and a half feet of Joyce criticism, and three quarters of a foot of Heinlein novels, please." We read not only the beat writers, but the modern, fast-paced ones like Herbert Gold, Philip Roth, and many others. We also read some `traditional' bohemians like Herman Hesse. Heuyman's *Against Nature* was an often praised work, as were all of the existentialist's writings. In fact, we read voraciously, and in almost every style and period, always including those works that were almost required reading for everyone in our generation; the short list (as opposed to the long one, which did exist) would include *On the Road, Stranger in a Strange Land, Siddartha, the Tin Drum,* all of Tolkin, *Brave New World,* and Marvel Comics. Biography, novel, film, painting, painting on film, filming on painting (I remember a delightful one on Picasso's mobiles), sculpture, music, dance, they penetrated us from every direction as if we were pin cushions and the pins were Eros of art.

Added together, the message that we sought, and received with intensity, was that life should be a sprawling, unpredictable, adventure, leading to either a glorious, early death, or to a wizardly serenity coupled with knowledge and power.

North Beach was anomalous in many ways; the whole Italian neighborhood-beatnik shops area was bordered on one side by a street called Broadway. Broadway was very level and straight. This street was San Francisco's weak imitation of 'Vegas: bright lights and garish signs, but defiantly, poor cousin. There were topless bars and nightclubs. Many a drunken tourist wandered around the corner and stumbled upon, often with a mixture of curiosity and disgust, the almost Magic Theater atmosphere of the real North Beach; the natives were friendly, if somewhat good-humoredly, condescending. "Hey, dad, better make it back to the hotel, you're not walking too good."

Another vehicle for transmission of 'the message', was folk music. In high school, I had listened to the Kingston Trio. As aspiring beats, we were drawn to what we considered to be authentic folk musics. I listened to Leadbelly, Robert Johnson, Woodie Guthrie, Brownie McGhee and Sonny

Terry, and others. I went to folk coffee houses and bars in San Francisco, New York, L.A., and many smaller towns such as San Diego and Santa Cruz. Mostly in the coffee houses, we heard middle class white people who were trying to absorb, or pretend they had absorbed, some kind of roots tradition. An exception was a pre-"Sounds of Silence" Simon and Garfunkle singing about being Jewish boys from the suburbs. I went to concerts by Odetta, Mariam Makeba, Ravi Shankar and others. I also liked Joan Baez, who had gone to high school near where I grew up. Friends of mine knew her, and told me that in high school, she often brought her guitar to parties, but that no one wanted to hear her; sounds like real life to me. When Bob Dylan came along, we felt incredibly fortunate; here was a folk artist of our own culture. Somehow, he conveyed authenticity, and we bought it. Some of his words were hard to understand as to specific meaning, but that just made the feeling stronger inside of us that the communication was hip and complete. If you had to ask what it meant, you obviously weren't capable of understanding it. In any case, the words on *the Freewheeling Bob Dylan* were pretty clear, and, at the same time, they set us up to embrace the more abstract words that were to come. Love was unrequited, parking meters were radioactive.

I was nineteen and Jerry and Grace were twenty four. One day they told me that their marriage was an open one; they both occasionally made it with other people. Around this same time, they started talking about marijuana which I had not tried. I was a little afraid, but I really wanted to try it. One day they invited me to dinner, and when I got there, they told me they had some.

"Where'd you get it?" I asked.

"Bought it from a cop over in Berkeley." said Jerry. "A lot of cops deal drugs on the side."

"How do you know he won't bust you?"

"Come on, Darb'," said Grace, "we met him through friends. Doug's been scoring from him for years."

By now, I was sweating, and shaking from nervousness; this was the stuff we had been taught would addict and kill you. Many people had recently described it to me as non-addictive, but I was still nervous. There was no way, however, that I wasn't going to try it. Grace handed me a tobacco pipe which was full of it; not a little marijuana on a special screen on top of the pipe, but a full-sized pipe, full of dope. I smoked it all and nothing happened. I smoked some more. Again, nothing. I smoked again. Suddenly, it hit me. I started laughing. I felt happy and free. We laughed and laughed about silly things, in fact most of the time none of us could even finish a sentence without laughing; we laughed so often that we could hardly talk. Grace had been cooking while I smoked. She had fixed spaghetti which she served with a little garlic salt, butter, and parmesan cheese. It tasted wonderful, the best thing I had ever eaten! Somehow, even the gasoline-like Red Mountain wine tasted delicious, its puckering astringency an asset. I never wanted to be without marijuana again. Walking home on the dark streets of San Francisco, I became afraid that I would be mugged or busted for the small amount of marijuana I was bringing home with me. These were reasonable fears, but blown into paranoia by the drug.

We said, and consciously thought, we wanted drugs to be experimental, not habitual. Next, we wanted to try peyote. A friend named Nigel had procured some for us from New Mexico or Arizona. As far as I know, it was legal for them to mail it to us in California at the time (not that illegality would have deterred us). We called Nigel "the mad scientist" which in some ways he was; by day he worked in a plastics lab, and by night he experimented on himself and his friends.

He boiled the plants and reduced them to a small amount of greenish brown liquid. He had set up a situation for taking the drug that was supposed to be pleasurable and uplifting, but like an experiment, complete with a straight person who would ask us prepared questions such as, "define the nature of God." Jerry, Grace, and I each drank about a tablespoon of the disgusting sludge, chased quickly with grapefruit juice to get rid of the taste, and it did taste awful. About fifteen minutes later, I began to feel somewhat ill at ease and confused. One by one, we vomited, and immediately after, the high arrived. There was no confusion. Everything seemed known, and in fact, taken for peaceful granted. Each time we closed our eyes, we saw beautiful colors transmuting through various crystal forms. Grace became very attracted to a large squash, which she then carried with her for six to eight hours. Our straight person played a record of Hindustani flute music which was profoundly beautiful to me; I seemed to feel eternity. Many kinds of music sounded trivial, as did the prepared questions which we answered with disdainful monosyllables.

Did we storm the gates of God consciousness with this drug? I don't know, but if so, "storm the gates" is the operative phrase; better to enter peaceably through the door of time.

Then came the Beatles.

Looking back on it now, I don't see how so many would-be musicians could have listened to the Beatles and said, "If they can do it, I can do it." but that's what happened. Almost all young people flipped out over the Beatles. An example: my brother Jerry left a party in San Francisco on the spur of the moment with some friends and drove to Long Beach to play the Beatles new album for friends there. The fact that, in their drunkenness, they had brought with them only the empty record jacket, did not show a lack of zeal. Grace, who had been left behind, phoned me and said, "Jerry's in Long Beach. 'Wanna drive down with me and get him?"

"Sure," I said, always grabbing any chance to be with her. When we arrived, the record was playing on the turntable (they had, upon discovering that the jacket was empty, rushed out and bought a new copy) and I think we listened to it non-stop for about three days before departing again for San Francisco.

That first Beatle album knocked many whole forms of music right off the road. Later, talking to my friends in various bands, some wouldn't admit to having been encouraged to form their groups by the success of the Beatles. I guess they just happened to like the same kind of boots and long hair.

In any case, many of us were cruising along playing music in bohemian living rooms, getting loaded, when the Beatles hit. Sometimes Grace and I played all night, she on the recorder, I on the acoustic guitar. We never played songs, only free, non-scalar improvisations, each one listening to the other and trying to add to the blend of melody, counterpoint, harmony, and rhythm. It is tempting to say that this music was all garbage, because of the drugs and alcohol, and I'm sure we did produce plenty of that, but I've heard some of the tapes we made, and some of this music has stood up for me through the years. Whether it was worth the price that would be paid, is another story. Jerry Garcia was in Palo Alto teaching guitar in a music store at this time. Janis was in Texas loving the blues. John Cipollina was in Mill Valley getting his Scottie Moore licks together.

B. Slick

Me and Jerry. Christmas, Palo Alto, 1947

B. Slick

Dan, Jerry and Darby Slick, 1950

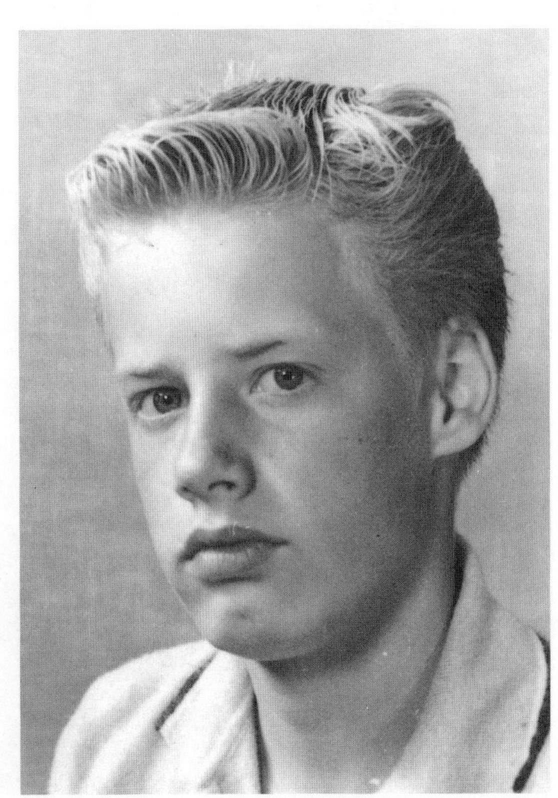

B. Slick

First day, Sr. High

B. Slick

Grace at my parent's beach house, 1965

J. Piersol

Grace & Carol Slick, 1965, Carol's birthday

2

Before Society

I think back to the year before we started our little band. Love, or rather the desire to escape from love, had driven me to New York. I didn't want to love her but she was in every thought, every plan, in even small considerations. If she talked of a movie she wanted to see, that movie became, other than she, the most important thing in the world. Listening to her talk, my mind drifted uncontrollably between her words and the ideas her words expressed, and the shape of her neck and the texture, and perhaps smell, of her skin. If she chanced to lean forward, I could listen to no word she said. She was so smart and beautiful, and so fucked-up.

Anything connected to Germany was obscene to her; she repeatedly, and ferociously, attacked a German-born friend of a friend we occasionally ran into at parties. He was an artist, a writer, who had left Germany because of a kind of national shame. On some interior level, I think he welcomed her attacks as vindicating his own self-hatred; it was not fun to watch, neither her part nor his. She was always drunk when this happened, but she was the most amazing drunk; only people who really knew her could tell she had been drinking. Right up to passing out, which she only rarely did, she appeared coordinated and clear of speech. It was just that she was so completely unreasonable, so completely without compassion. Later, she might have no memory of what had transpired.

Her mind leapt with dizzying speed, what is normally called jumping to conclusions. Sometimes this was brilliant intuition, sometimes mere stupidity. It did not seem to matter to her; she inhabited whatever new position with her entire being. It was like watching a person jump from square to square on a chessboard made of transmogrifiers.

She had a freckled face, which she covered with the heavy make-up she had learned to apply as a model. Not what you'd think of as an outdoors person, she was nonetheless peeling on her nose from the hours she spent gardening daily; she had filled her back yard with marijuana plants which she had grown from seed. The elderly Italian landlady who lived next door, often stuck her head over the fence, and chatted with her while she scrupulously weeded around the tall plants. The landlady was not an overly kind or liberal person; although she never asked about the plants, I'm sure that if she had thought they were marijuana, she would have instantly telephoned the police.

All in all, while I loved every part of her, and she certainly was attractive, it was her mind that set her apart. The searing quickness of her thinking, the insistence on learning whatever interested her, now, the combination of intellect and romanticism that made Lewis Carrol, Rimsky-Korsakov, and Aldous Huxley favorites of hers, were all lovable aspects. Nonetheless, love is like a fetish in that we are hard-pressed to know why we like a particular person, or shoe, so much.

The same attributes that enabled her to exchange solos in the call and response style so brilliantly, served her exceedingly well in conversation, except, of course, when she was drunk. Talking with her, one often felt that the conversation reached the level of wit of an Oscar Wilde play. Unlike Wilde, however, she seemed to have little patience with homosexuality; A bi-sexual male friend of mine, once called her the coldest person he had ever met. Other mutual gay friends described her as kind. How to reconcile these views? I think her affections were like lasers, extremely directional, and with little side-splash. The went where they were pointed with brutal, if sometimes ill-considered, accuracy.

Her visual art skills were acute. One time she wrote a movie script by drawing astonishing little story-board pictures of each camera angle. She made beautiful little paper models of guitars and angels as Christmas tree ornaments. She did a watercolor picturing me as an old man in which I clearly resembled myself, but with many of the attributes of Bertrand Russell; I can't imagine flattery that could have worked better on me.

I will tell you some stories of her; I am aware that they fit more into the category of "loving her, warts and all" than they do into the heroic, but all of these events endeared her to me.

One time, Jerry and Grace and I went to Santa Cruz to visit Jerry and my parents at their beach house. The house was large and rather boring. The living room was painted white and was sparsely decorated with expensive items picked by a San Francisco, Union Street decorator who catered to people who liked bland. Grace and my mother and I began to drink heavily. My father and Jerry gradually drifted off to their beds. The three of us who remained, began to discuss politics and money. My mother, a Republican, was all for wealth and privilege, and the concern she had for humanity was essentially of the noblesse oblige variety. Grace and I were for socialism and the revolution-art process. At one point, my mother began to take off her large diamond ring and give it to Grace, saying something like, "You're young. Wait 'till you have some nice things and then see how you feel about socialism." Grace replied, "If you give me that ring, I'll walk straight out to the edge of the cliff and throw it in the ocean." My mother hurriedly shoved the ring back on her finger. Getting drunker, Grace and I began to complain about bourgeois values, and particularly about the house. My mother challenged her to improve it if she could, so Grace got out a box of charcoals and began drawing on a large wall. Soon, I joined her, and at some point, we moved on to drawing on the ceiling as well. I had no visual art skills, so my own contribution was ugly in the extreme, but I did manage to remember some lines from *The Love Song of J. Alfred Prufrock* which I gladly added to the jumble. It was fun and somewhat liberating, if also somewhat sophomoric, and not entirely unlike a scene from *The Horse's Mouth*. The next day, as we reeled, terribly hung-over, into the living room, Grace suddenly excused herself and ran to the bath room to vomit. My stomach was also very rocky. Only my mother who, by this time, had drunk alcoholically for many years, seemed her usual self. She was amused by the look of the house. It was indicative of the power that was growing in the hippies, that my parents had at least one party in this room before they had it painted white again. The last time I visited this house, I could still see traces of our art work through what must have been at least the third paint job. It may be that every generation thinks it can change the world, but God, we were so convinced, and for a while, it really started to happen. Lawyers, judges and senators began smoking dope and dropping acid; things that had been totally unacceptable, became fashionable. You may know these things already, but I'm trying to get you to feel, possibly not for the first time, the power of it, the momentum. It looked as if the whole old culture, which to us had become a kind of anti-culture, would be thrown off the cliff into the ocean. Unprecedented change is as exciting as driving a Ferrari through mountain curves; anything might happen, you're not fastened down on a track at Disneyland. Now, in the early nineties, with all the changes in the world, we are getting another taste of this rapid, unpredictable change and, again, it is exciting and terrifying.

Another time, Jerry and Grace and I were invited to a party given by some friends of theirs on the peninsula (just south of San Francisco). These were high school friends who were not part of the new scene. They were frightened by it and by us, but they were also curious. They had rented an empty warehouse and had hired Lou Rawls to play. We brought George Hunter of the Charlatans with us, don't ask me why. George had the longest hair of any man I had seen up to that time, and he was heavily into image. His tight black jeans and Victorian cowboy jacket set off his long blond hair and made a "look at me" statement. The locals looked and hated. As the evening progressed, and people began to get drunk, comments became uglier and more threatening. George didn't say much; his conversation in this time period, that is, for these few years, consisted almost entirely of, "Well, you know, man." It had become somewhat of a joke among the various band people, and George, ever an able observer, seemed to accept his conversational role with dignity and humor. Sometimes he only uttered parts of his phrase, as in, "You know," or, "Man, man." Grace, on the other hand, though drunk, was not at a loss for words. She egged on the drunken capitalists with her drunken socialist remarks. The only thing worse to these folks than long hair was a commie, and they had never pondered the difference between communism and socialism; sometimes it seemed they had never pondered anything. Soon, several of the meanest had decided to cut off George's hair. They were not joking. One pulled a knife, and the others made to grab George and hold him down. Grace picked up a wine bottle and, holding it by the neck, began to beat it on the table, the pillars and the floor, trying to fashion a weapon for herself; the bottle would not break. As the crowd's attention turned away from George and towards "this crazy broad", the tension dissipated, and, after a little while, we were able to get out of there. Grace didn't want to leave. She was really angry, mostly at the bottle, by now, for refusing to break. Within a year, many of the people at this party were trying to pretend that they had always been "hip", and virtually all were making efforts to show that they were at least somewhat "with it."

One of Jerry's high school sweethearts, Irma, had married a man named Doug. Doug stood out in any crowd. His I.Q. was enormous, and his mind was very facile, a noteworthy quality even in our group of friends, most of whose minds were considered to be in the genius category. As a child, Doug had been a Quiz Kid. He was at least somewhat crazy, and he loved most drugs. He was about three years older than Jerry and Grace, and had been on the drug scene a few years when we were introduced to it. Doug loved to listen to Christian radio hucksters who were always trying to raise money by "giving away" prayer cloths and other things, in exchange for contributions. Doug was extremely political, in a left wing way, and he taught me a lot about arguing. A favorite game, was to try to slowly twist an argument around until each was arguing the other's point. Doug, who had been raised Jewish, had essentially abandoned religion, but he still refused to eat pork; his wife used to try to sneak pork-fat into the cooking sometimes because she believed it made him more horny. She told us that one time, while high on some psychedelic drug, he had stood on top of their little radio and urinated in a circular pattern as a sort of benediction. Grace liked, or loved, Doug, and she and I spent a lot of time with him. He used to shoot heroin occasionally, always stopping after two days so as not to become addicted. In a very un-pushy way, he offered to turn us on to it too, if we wanted, but we were afraid of needles. I did, however, buy from him a one quart can, similar to a paint can, that was full of the little beads of benzedrine (speed) that go into capsules. From the drugstore, I bought some empty capsules, and began taking this speed daily. Soon, I didn't bother with the capsules, but just stuck a spoon into the can and ate as much as I wanted. I shared with some friends, and sold a little to others. Doug had such a complicated personality, and he so enjoyed thinking of himself as the consummate con artist, that five years later, when he went completely straight and began to manage one of the bay area's largest sports facilities, I didn't know what to think of him; he only smiled faintly when the old days were mentioned, and he looked and talked like an insurance salesman. Where was the old Doug? I couldn't find out. He seemed to have undergone the transformation referred to in *Harvey*, but I always thought that the old Doug was inside that mind somewhere, laughing and biding his time. He was the first person I saw display the poster "I Want Magic", and I wanted it also.

A friend named Roy began to have weekly parties. Actually, Roy began to have parties lasting, in some way, all weekend, every weekend. Friday nights, he would cook gourmet dinners for ten to twelve people, three of whom were almost always Jerry, Grace and I. Saturday night was party night, and it was virtually an open house. Sunday was recovery day, which meant drugs and alcohol, but low key. On Saturday nights, many people would come, including, often, a few celebrity artists of various fields. The living room action was relatively straight, with music and conversation, cigarettes and drinks. More than once, Grace dominated the living room festivities with her impassioned speeches. Her specialty: ranting fascistically about fascism. Her behavior was so easy to parody, so absurd; "Let's line-up all the war mongers and kill them." Certainly, I was at no higher level of sophistication than she. She often seemed brave and insightful to me; I was drunk too.

Outside the house in the small yard, and downstairs in the little sitting room, some intense drug scenes took place. Sometimes, several of us would smoke magic mushrooms through a water pipe, while sitting on Roy's blue Scandinavian couch. Occasionally, the room disappeared, and I entered strange mental worlds of abstract colors and vibrating shapes. Returning to consciousness of my body and of the room could be surprising, in the way that it can be surprising to look up from a novel, and discover that you are not in the place described in the book. Once, I became very frightened when, in a "dream", I let go of a handle, which, to me, represented reality, and I watched it shoot away at high speed, forever un-recoverable, as I thought. An hour or so later, I was okay, but I remained upset for days.

When the movie, *Lawrence of Arabia* came out, Grace had to see it immediately. I think Peter O'Toole was the prime attraction to her, as he was to many others. She loved the movie; was fascinated by the cinematography, the music, the acting and the story. Next, she bought the soundtrack album, and T. E Lawrence's autobiography, *The Seven Pillars of Wisdom*. For a year or so, it seemed that whenever I visited them, I heard that Hollywood desert music. Lest I come off as "better than" here, I must add that I shared all of these fascinations with Grace, and even today, I still love fake, desert music.

Much of what I can say about say about Grace and me, would be true for many young would-be lovers. For one thing, we looked the part. In fact, my brother spent several whole afternoons posing us for still photos as lovers in Golden Gate Park, in a large convertible, and by some abandoned railroad tracks. The tensions of our unconsummated love were palpable, even in photographs. We never touched. I was much too jumpy; the few times Grace touched me, I leapt as if from an electric shock. I think Grace was drawn to me, and was also flattered that I was so completely obsessed by her. My brother continued to love Grace, but he also saw other women at this time. More and more, she and I shut him out of our deep moods. Most of my life I have loved, liked and respected my brother; he is handsome, smart, has a wonderful sense of humor and a great rhythmic talent. During this period, however, my desire for Grace overshadowed my love for him. Often, he returned to their house late at night to find Grace and me drunk, stoned, and playing abstract, fragmented music on our instruments. Not touching each other caused us to touch in music. We poured ourselves through our instruments, and our musical phrases did what our bodies did not do. I think Grace was willing, but I couldn't get past the fact that she was married to my brother. As it turned out, she had the same inhibition. The tensions grew. She became verbally abusive towards Jerry, often calling him a Nazi and other terrible things, though she half disguised her abuse as a joke. Finally, the afternoon arrived when Jerry didn't come home and a very drunk, but to me infinitely desirable, Grace offered herself to me. I had dreamed of something like this, but had not really thought that it would happen. I wanted her, but it was very difficult for me to accept that she could want me. She had shown strong signs of wanting me, but I just couldn't let it in. I was incredulous. I said something like, "You mean you really want....." and she said, "Of course, but every time I touched you, you practically jumped out of your skin and away from me."

We knew we shouldn't stay there, so we decided to drive to Jerry and my parent's house which was unoccupied at the time, and for which I had a key. We got into the car and I started driving towards Santa Cruz. Grace immediately wanted to stop to buy more alcohol. I hesitated, and she said, "You don't get it. I can't do this thing without booze." I understood that she meant that she couldn't make it with *me* without alcohol, not that she always had to be drunk. It was then that I knew that her inhibitions were as strong as mine. I stopped in some little neighborhood, at some little store, and bought her some cheap champagne, and myself some beer. We proceeded, but ended up driving almost the whole way on local streets and we stopped at least twice more for booze. Every half hour or so, we smoked a fat joint.

We arrived at the beach sometime after dark, and I let us into the large, empty house. The air in the living room was still hot and stale from the day, and the three old clocks chimed quarter hourly until I stopped them. The large iguana in the sun room thrashed about occasionally in his private jungle, his blood still warm enough from the afternoon to allow him intense, rapid movement. I had left a few records at the house, so I picked out one by Ravi Shankar and put it on the turntable. Neither of us was anxious to begin this thing that we had committed to do, so Grace said that she wanted a shower, and that she would meet me back in the living room. I went off to a different bathroom to shower. Some time later, we meet again in the living room, each wearing only underpants. We lay down on the floor and began to kiss and fondle. We were both very tense, in spite of massive amounts of alcohol and pot. We began to copulate, but soon I became limp, and Grace was also obviously little aroused. We hugged and went to sleep.

Morning brought bursting hangovers, with Grace vomiting, and much confusion. She did not remember much of what had happened; she had been in an alcoholic blackout. It was obvious to her that we had had sex, but she didn't remember leaving San Francisco, or the trip to Santa Cruz. I don't think her feelings towards me had changed, she was very tender with me, and I know that I still loved her, but it seemed time to go back to San Francisco and life as we had known it.

Arriving back in the city, we saw that Jerry had not returned home. I left to go sleep in my little rented room in the rooming house run by the old sea captain whose own place was decorated with wooden round-topped chests and prayer rugs from Istanbul and Alexandria. Milk and cheese in the cooler made from an old slatted California Apricot box outside my window had rotted, and my dirty room, with its stiff, mold-smelling sheets on the chipped yellow-white painted metal bed was a gloomy, narrowing sight to me. My desk was messy with overdue library books on math theory and music and pages on which I had drawn grids of musical note-names. I'd superimpose geometric shapes on the grids as a way of generating melodies. This trick, I had learned from John Cage's book, *Silences*. I dropped onto the bed, and fell off to sleep dreaming of Grace.

I didn't want to try to break up her marriage to my brother, and I didn't want to live and work in close proximity to them; I had to get out. My friend Lawrence, the same guy I had visited on my first day in the army, had become bi-coastal, in a poor man's sort of way, and he was leaving to spend his summer in New York. Lawrence was the only son of Mexican emigrants. He was bi-sexual. He hated all things Mexican and refused to speak Spanish with his family. When he was about sixteen, his parents took him to Mexico to visit relatives, and he dressed the whole time in penny loafers with white socks, Bermuda shorts, a Hawaiian shirt, and kept a camera constantly slung around his neck. Less than ten years later, at the age of thirty five, he would die from the effects of alcohol and drug abuse.

Lawrence...

Tahlula Bunkhead slammed back four green hearts and halfa glass of watery, melted-ice scotch and lit another filter tip by placing the cigarette in her mouth backward. The smell bothered me, but didn't seem greatly to disturb her, although she did put it out quickly in the overflowing, black disk ashtray with it's outer ring of tiny, black-ball cigarette holders.

The walls of her room were covered inch by inch with posters, collages which she had made herself, and which were very good, free associating as they did both visually and by subject, oh anything eye catching, a pink feather boa next to a plastic boa constrictor. A pith helmet next to a urinal, an asshole next to the planet of the same name (not mine!). One of the two beds in the small, crowded room was piled four feet high in "things". Magazines, the better to collage you with, little plastic toys, a million items any one of which would be forgettable, but knowing Tahlula, you knew why she had saved it and you valued it too. You couldn't clean the place, you just had to step back and watch it grow, hoping that nothing virulent would crop up. There was an ironic suspense always in the air, as if something had just happened, would happen or was happening now. Did you know it? Was it something you'd really want to know? Maybe not.

There was smoke, too, and dust. Smells made complicated by new perfumes, and an orange turned green with white fringes.

It was three A.M., that time when the choice must be made to say good night, or to join in the green heart, pill paved road to reason without intellectual burden, synapses firing across new routes unhindered bysequential logic. This was what she lived for, the out times when life was more, or less, than supermarket smiles, but the darker side of it alarmed even her, though she foolishly committed to it in advance, swearing not to be deterred by the very things which are meant to deter us. It isn't blame I feel for her, but sadness that she couldn't make the course corrections. It's okay to try walking on your head, but when you know that it is scuffing your brain, that's the time for shoes!

Lawrence had repeatedly offered to show me New York, and I decided to take him up on it. I hitch-hiked across the country in the late spring of '64. I took a small, private room in the Brooklyn Y.M.C.A., and waited for

Lawrence to show up. For the first time in my life, I got a feeling for why anybody would want to watch a baseball game when I saw sand lot teams play in Brooklyn parks on Sunday afternoons. It kept reminding me of the turn of the century, and of the songs that were popular then, and of things like "follow the bouncing ball". I was not the only one to feel the time warp; when I rented a little too hot, too cold apartment almost directly under the Brooklyn Bridge, my landlady asked me if we were having much trouble with wild Indians in California, and if I had had to cross dangerous seas to get to New York. Did she think that I had chosen to go around the Horn, rather than come by covered wagon?

I did all the things that a young would-be artist did in New York at the time. I went to art galleries, loft parties, poetry readings on Village piers, was introduced to many successful actors and painters, read *A Tale of Two Cities*, and *The Alexandria Quartet.*

When *A Hard Day's Night* came out, it didn't play Manhattan or even, I think, Brooklyn. Lawrence and I had to ride for hours on subways to get to where it was playing.

"This better be worth it." he said, as we bounced along in the dirty train.

"You love their music as much as I do. Jesus Christ, how many times have we played the guitar all night long without playing a single song by anybody else. And you're the one whose records we've fucked-up scratching the needle back to the beginning of each song a million times so we could figure out the fucking chord changes, man."

"It's not like you have to convince me. I've been coming to New York for half of each year for ah...three years, and you know I don't stay home a lot. But shit, I've never been anywhere near where this movie is playing, and that bothers me some."

We finally got off the train in some innocuous neighborhood almost all of whose stridently middle-class stores were already closed for the evening, and made our way to the theater. Inside, we found people much like ourselves: young art-types. The attitude of the movie was completely reflective of the people I knew. Fuck authority with a smile on your face. This revolution would throw no bombs, but it would take few prisoners.

Lenny Bruce was not a friend of mine, but I admired him greatly. He talked about things that were important to me: sex, politics, hypocrisy. I couldn't believe that he was being hassled for using "bad" words. There is little point in going deeply into the merits of his court case here, but certainly time has vindicated him, and has made the judges who ruled against him appear laughable and bigoted. I had heard some of his early records, and had seen him in nightclub performances. When I heard that he was on trial in New York, I decided at once to attend.

It was sunny and hot as I walked toward the large gray court building. I walked up to the hot dog stand on the street with its colorful cafe-style umbrella, and joined the noontime crowd of hungry people. As I ate my hotdog, I watched people stream out of the court building and into the large open-doored bar on the corner. Many knew each other, and their faces bespoke years of hard-drinking lunches. They looked, to me, like lawyers and judges; in any case, they didn't wonder where to go, but headed straight for the bar. At about one o'clock, I walked into the court building, and found a clerk to tell me where the trial was being held. I rode up in the old elevator which smelled of disinfectant, and got off on the third floor.

Inside the courtroom, all of the participants except the three judges were already in place. Lenny was sitting with his lawyer, and they were talking quietly, but I could see by his face and hand waving that Lenny was very agitated. The bailiff made his, "All rise!" speech, we did, and in walked Larry, Curly, and Moe.

Looking around the large room, I didn't see any other "fans" at the trial. There were a few people watching, but they seemed like retired people who probably would come every day and just try to pick the most interesting trial in the building.

Lenny was really distraught because he was being treated so unfairly. I watched as his act was presented to the three judges by cops in such a garbled fashion, that only a stream of "obscenities" remained. The cops, reading from what they claimed were transcriptions of tape recordings they had made of Lenny's live act, intoned in sing-song voices statements like, "Goddamn, motherfucker, fuck you in the ass, motherfucker, shit shit shit." The prosecutor then argued that the act had no redeeming social value. Lenny was beside himself. Also, he had learned a lot about the law, and clearly felt that he was being poorly represented. After the day's session, I rode down in the elevator with Lenny and his lawyer.

"They're killing me in there," said Lenny, "you've got to let me give them an idea of what my act is really like, and they're doin' all kinds of bullshit, illegal stuff to me why don't you stop them?" I couldn't hear the lawyer's reply, but it didn't seem to satisfy Lenny.

I returned daily for the trial; it was awful, but I couldn't stay away. Watching this mighty, swift, and compassionate man being attacked by the representatives of our society was deeply disturbing to me; I had known of how haughty many judges are, but I was shocked that they would make such fools of themselves "on the record".

Gradually, the summer heat began to lessen, and a beautiful fall set in. As this season progressed, however, I began to freeze at night in my apartment. The law required landlords in New York to turn on the heat on a certain day each year, and I eagerly awaited it. When it came, I realized that the amount of heat my old radiator would provide would be insufficient. I was sleeping at night with several pairs of pants on, and several shirts, and a jacket, and with blankets and a plastic bag over me, but still I was cold all night. I decided to go back to California. Lawrence and I and two other friends set out in a drive-away car. I wondered if I was over my love for Grace and wanted to test it; if I needed to live in a different city than she, at least I would pick a warm one. We drove straight across the country, taking speed and driving in shifts, each sleeping a little. We drank very little, and had smoked the last of our dope, even down to the dreaded crushed seeds, before leaving New York.

Jerry and Grace had written to me that they had moved to a beautiful little white house overlooking the bay in Tiburon (just north of San Francisco), so we drove right there. They weren't home, but they had left the door open for us. In the 'fridge were several six packs of beer. On Jerry's big wooden desk was a Norwegian cookie can about an inch deep in sifted pot with rolling papers on top. On the turntable was the Rolling Stones' brand-new-just-released 12 By 5, and on the refrigerator door was a note inviting us to enjoy all of these things, and saying that they would be home in a few hours; we did.

I was back.

3

Our First Gig

Seeing Grace, I realized that I still loved her, but was not "in love" with her. I felt very relieved. Soon, I rented a room from Nigel the mad scientist in his San Francisco house near the Haight-Ashbury District. He gave a large party, an open-house to all who heard of it, and there I ran into a young woman I had met before named Leslie. She had previously lived with a friend of mine, Peter Van Gelder. Peter was a musician, and he was a handsome and magnetic person. The fact that Leslie had lived with Peter gave her added appeal to me (I'm not bragging about this). She was very smart and pretty, and had lived with drugs and self-imposed poverty longer than I. She had a stoic attitude about the hard knocks of life, and she wore very short skirts. Being nineteen or twenty, we both had the bursting auras of barely ripened fruit. We fell in love.

Leslie and I rented a second floor (second of two) flat in the Mission District of San Francisco. This flat was surrounded on all four sides by garden and, as we were on the top floor, the feeling was of living in a large tree house; on sunny days, and there were many, our home was fairy-tale beautiful.

During this time, Jerry, Grace, and I, formed what would evolve into our band, the Great Society. Jerry had gotten a degree in cinematography from San Francisco State. While there, he had met and worked with many people who would become participants in the San Francisco music scene. One of them, Bill Piersol, was a friend from Palo Alto who majored in English at State. He wrote the script that Jerry directed as his final student project. Grace wrote and performed the music for this film. Bill had married a beautiful young mostly-Italian woman named Jean, another high school friend from a town just south of Palo Alto, and she could really sing.

Jerry set up our old pink and black drum set, and bought Grace a shiny red Japanese electric guitar. I went to visit them, and naturally picked up the guitar and started playing. Jerry sat down at the drums, joined in, and we were off! It was so fun. They had set up some cheap microphone and plugged it into the stereo. Grace started singing over my Chuck Berry-inspired guitar chords. It was like Judy Garland and Mickey Rooney, "Hey, why don't we do the show right here!" Jerry and Grace must have thought of forming a band, but they hadn't told me; they let me discover the joy of it for myself. The idea of playing music every day seemed so fun that it should be illegal, but they were saying yes, we get to.

I went to Sears and bought myself a Silvertone electric guitar. These Silvertones were made by Danelectro, and today are highly sought after. The pickups were wound by hand, and each one sounded different. The one I picked, had a particularly thonky, raunchy sound, which I loved.

Jerry and Grace asked Jean if she wanted to sing with us, and since she was a Beatlemaniac, she didn't hesitate.

We started to rehearse. We had two electric guitars, drums, no bass, and Grace and Jean sang. Grace wrote all of the first few songs. She made lyric sheets of the five or so songs she had written and, having no music holder, she taped them to a lamp stand. One of the earliest was "Father Bruce", of course about Lenny Bruce. Grace recounted Lenny's fall out of the window of the Swiss Hotel in North Beach; anybody who falls out of windows must be okay, right? She extolled the virtues of Lenny, while criticizing the hypocrisy that was then so rampant. The fifties had just ended, and very many people insisted on presenting a sort of Norman Rockwell public persona, but few private lives were actually that straight. Our friend from the San Francisco State days, Ray Andersen, had become a friend of Lenny's at this time, and we were always getting the latest inside stories. Grace had gone to college with Jill St. John, so Grace had some entree to Hollywood, but Lenny represented a different kind of celebrity, a sort of people's intellectual.

Three days a week or more, I would leave my Mission District flat and drive over to Twin Peaks to pick up Jean. She and I would then drive across the Golden Gate Bridge to Tiburon. On our way in, we would stop at a large quonset-styled grocery store and I would buy us a bottle of vodka for the rehearsal. We would then drive past a large grassy field in which stood Blackie, the most sway-backed horse I have ever seen. Blackie stood in this field for many years, and when he died, the field was given to the town, and was officially named McKaren's Meadow; it was unfortunate that they named it that, because no one I know will ever call it anything but Blackie's Pasture.

These rehearsal days were ecstatic for me. I would leave my beautiful woman, to ride with another beautiful woman (with whom I gladly would have made it, if she hadn't been too wise to get involved with me) and go play music with yet another beautiful woman. I loved the alcohol, the marijuana, the women, the music, and I got along well with my brother at this time, also.

My first songs were jokes; I was getting my feet wet, without risk, by not calling what I did art. I think the first song I wrote was a silly surfer parody;

When I get you down to the ocean,
there will be a commotion,
all the surfers there will pearl (the noses of their boards will catch disastrously in the waves),
when they hear that you're my girl,
they've had their eyes on you so long."

I also wrote a minor-chorded tune that Grace named "Dirge". Jerry wrote a song called "Born to Be Burned", which we continued to play for some time.

I don't remember who introduced us to it, but one day one of us had received some L.S.D., which was just starting to be known in our area. I think we had read some discussions of celebrity usage of it, perhaps by

Alpert and Leary and Aldous Huxley, and we were certainly primed to take it. Jean didn't come along, but I drove over to Jerry and Grace's house, and we "dropped acid". Soon, we were literally crawling around on our hands and knees, both inside the house, and outside, where we crawled to a little dirt mound and lost ourselves in its tall grass and bushes. Every bug and every leaf was fascinating, impossible. The wet dirt was intense and alive and I wanted to rub it on my face. Perhaps I did. Jerry and Grace seemed like strange creatures to me, and we all seemed like astronauts from some other planet. I remember odd-looking neighbors giving us odd looks as we crawled back up the path into the little white house, but for some reason, no one called the cops. Later, we learned we had taken massive doses of L.S.D., and that was why we had been unable to walk. Jerry and Grace had a large white Persian cat that they had taken to calling Walt, the essence-sound of their original name, Quality (Cat), and while high, Grace did an oil painting of their living room in which the most prominent features were her red electric guitar, and Walt. For her canvas, she choose Jerry's bass drum head, and Jerry used it for most of the Great Society gigs.

One day, Jean tearfully announced that she and her husband were moving to San Jose, where they would receive free rent in her mother's large house, and Bill would work on a novel. We didn't want her to go, but there was nothing we could do. For a short time, we put our band on hold. Jerry and Grace then moved to a house in Larkspur, about five miles north of Tiburon. We set up the equipment in the boomy, wooden-floored living room, and started blasting; now we were a trio, still with no bass, and I was singing a few songs, and doing backing parts on a few others.

We knew we needed more people, and we found them in two friends, David Minor, and Bard Dupont. David sang, played rhythm guitar and wrote songs, and Bard played bass and harmonica. Grace and David began working on vocal duet versions of each of their songs, and again, we were practicing regularly. The Tiburon house had been on a green hillside, way outside of town, and the police had never come, but in Larkspur, we were only one block from the main drag, and the police station was in that connecting block; they often interrupted our rehearsals with warnings to play quieter or, sometimes, with orders to stop altogether. The police, however, never mentioned drug use, no matter how recently we had smoked a joint or how strongly the house smelled of marijuana. Individual cops often told us that they loved our music and if Grace would smile and keep her mouth shut, we were home free.

David was handsome, and he had a great smile. He worked for the phone company, which he hated, and he was very ambitious; that was a new quality to us, because, until we meet him, we had just been floating along, hoping, almost even expecting, big things to happen. He looked at music more as a bossiness (sic) than we had, although I don't in any way imply that he didn't also value art. We started to ask ourselves questions like, "Gee, do you think we should do something to get our names out there?" As it happens, we almost didn't need to bother, because seldom has it happened that anyone was more in the right place at the right time.

The president's name was Lyndon Johnson, and we hated him; we had gone to hear the Beatles play, but someone had ax murdered them all, so the promoter was presenting Kate Smith instead. Who could have followed Jack Kennedy? Later, I would see Kennedy's picture in shoe shine stands in Istanbul, and on shop walls in India. Johnson seemed the prototypical southern politician, essentially dirty. We hated his personality, let alone his ideas. His plan of wonderment for America was called the Great Society, so we took this name, and said, 'We, we hippie-freak, drug addicts, we are your Great Society.' A few people didn't understand, and thought we were stuck up, which of course we were, but not in the unsubtle way of calling ourselves "great" publicly. It was an ugly name to us, like calling yourself dog shit, and we wore it with a sense of "fuck you to Madison Avenue." When the nation started to be fed publicity about the San Francisco hippies, it was presented with a picture of a bunch of cute and loving people, but there was a darker side. It was easy to push names like the Jefferson Airplane, and the Sopwith Camel, but what to make of the Grateful Dead? Actually, almost all hippie band people wanted changes so sweeping that they would be tantamount to revolution; drugs, and a kind of passive resistance, rather than guns, would be the instruments of the rebellion. We would not try to topple your society, we would simply walk away, figuratively, and build our own. Yours would blow itself up, or collapse from having all of its weight in the facade.

I had known a guy named John Carpenter for a year or so by 1965. Peter Van Gelder had introduced me to him. I had taken a lot of drugs with John, and we had often sat around for hours listening to the latest records and talking about everything we could think of to talk about. He was at loose ends, and when he started hearing about our band, he became interested in managing us.

John and I were in his Castro area apartment listening to Bob Dylan sing his new song about the unknowledgable Mr. Jones.
The place was a total mess; dirty dishes, books and records were everywhere. Crumpled, and presumedly soiled, clothes escaped sausage-like from the closet floor. John and I sat in chairs too tall for the old round oak table in front of us. The only clean place in the whole room was John's little dope area in front of him. He had been sieving marijuana onto Dylan's new album, and had rolling papers and three vastly different pipes lined up next to it.

"Dylan's so hip," laughed John, "his shit keeps getting better and better. Even the Beatles and the Stones are in awe of him."

"Yeh man." I was really stoned.

John was too, but the fat joint we had smoked only seemed to twist his thinking, not slow him down at all.

"You guys are really cool," he continued, "and we've got to make sure that every picture, every quote, every word of every poster, including the art style, shows people how hip you are." He was talking a mile a minute, and his eyes had the gleam of a megalomaniac. I loved it because he was talking about us.

It was part of those times that, of course, when we had needed a manager, we hadn't turned to a professional, but to a friend. John had curly blond hair, a slight lisp, and a quick mind. He laughed easily, but he could be moody as well, and he had a lot of doubts about himself as a person, and about his future; he worried a lot. His parents were pressuring him to do the straight thing: continue in college, get a high paying job. I should have seen the problem coming, but I didn't. I have always been inclined to wishful thinking. I want something to be all right, and feel that, somehow if I don't think about it, it will be. Anyway, in the case of John, I liked him, and I wanted him to be able to do the job he so obviously wanted to do. He was full of plans for the band, and made a very persuasive salesperson.

When we had agreed to do our first gig for the Family Dog, we asked John to set up a sort of shake-down gig for us. We didn't want the Family Dog show, which immediately looked big, to be our first time out. After long discussions of which places would be coolest to play, John called up a friend of his at the Coffee Gallery in North Beach and spoke to him about us.

The Coffee Gallery was a typical little, narrow, beat club that featured folk music and poetry readings. The place had prestige, but wasn't too intimidating. Business hadn't been that great lately. By this time, the beat movement was contracting as the hippie scene was getting going. The club was open to trying a new thing, and John assured them that we were it. I see him as the world's youngest Willie Loman, tap dancing for his friends, hustling us, and inside going, "shit, I don't know." Part of the problem that would develop, was that John was a friend of ours, and he was a friend of the club's manager. John was pulled both ways; he wanted the place to like us, and us to like the place, and he was paranoid about it all. His paranoia took the form of extreme tension.

The afternoon of the gig, October 15, 1965, we drove over, and set up. We were all nervous, but John started to really flip-out. He kept asking questions about our preparedness; "Is the guitar amp working? Do you know the order of the songs? Are you sure the guitar amp's working?" He was driving us crazy. As the time for our first set approached, he went into a full-blown identity crisis. He couldn't stop pacing, actually stalking, around the club. He was bothering everyone in the band; I had to get him out of there.

"Hey John," I said, smiling and shaking my head towards the door, "lets go for a walk."

"Now?" his eyebrows were pulled high on his forehead. There was no hint of humor about his mouth.

"Yes, now. Come on, I gotta talk to you." We headed out the door, into the North Beach night. The blocks were short, and the narrow streets were lined with beatnik shops, most of which were closed. I was so into our mental world that I was all but oblivious to our surroundings. Nonetheless, I remember that at one point, we stood at the top of a little hill and looked down on the thick, wavy-topped fog which covered the bay waters. I ended up walking around outside with him for about an hour, assuring and reassuring him that things would be okay, that he would be okay, and that he should try to calm down. Occasionally, I thought to myself, "Wow, this is really far out. Here it is my first gig, and instead of my manager helping me over my anxieties, I'm out trying to get *him* to relax."

We walked back to the club, I joined the others, and we played our first set. John sat in the back and listened, I guess; I could barely see him. We had grown so used to the acoustics in Jerry and Grace's Larkspur house, that it was hard for us to play in this club. Since it was our first time playing in a different room, we didn't understand what was wrong; everything, all of the instruments, and all of the song-sections sounded strange. Afterwards, John walked up towards us shaking his head in many directions, twitching yes no maybe, and smiled, "You guys were really great." I knew we weren't, but I thanked him for saying so. He looked really drained emotionally.

The audience reaction was mixed. About half of the people were regulars, and they didn't want to see their club go electric. Still, Grace's flute playing, and our obvious jazz influence seemed to sway them in our direction. The other half were drawn by our flyers, and they seemed instantly to like us. I still have one of those flyers, and Jerry is billed as 'electric percussionist', but that was just someone's fantasy, probably John's. We had heard examples of music in which industrial machines, such as oil wells, and drill presses, supplied the rhythmic sounds. We all liked this stuff, and wanted to do some ourselves, but, when it came down to it, we didn't; Jerry played a plain, old, (pink and black) drum set.

After the gig was over, the others called me aside, and told me something I already knew; John was too fucked-up to function as our manager. He was a nice guy, but he was going through so much interior searching and questioning, and drug abuse, that he couldn't just relax, and do the job. Next, followed an aspect of being a musician that I hate to this day. I had brought John to the band. I was the band leader. I had to fire him. John made it easy on me, he seemed to expect to be fired, but I hate this part of music. Once you're sure that things are not working out, you must separate from that person, otherwise, neither of you will grow. It can be very difficult determining, for sure, that things are not working out, and it can be heart-wrenching firing, or being fired. What we're talking about here, has more to do with love and dreams, than it does jobs; unfortunately, it also often has a lot to do with wishful thinking and denial. And, it sometimes happens that later, you can't remember why it seemed so important to get away from a particular person, or you remember your reasons, but, in the case of fellow-musicians, sometimes the tapes don't seem to bear you out: hard, weird, stuff.

John and I remained friendly, but we didn't see each other as often. He went through a period of working for the Family Dog with Chet and did some other local, but big time in their way, things. By 1967, he was living in Southern California, and writing rock and roll articles for the L.A. Free Press. This work made good use of his excellent descriptive abilities, and his non-musician's critical perspective. I saw him at the Monterey Pop Festival, where he was working as a reporter, and a short time later, I learned that he had been murdered while hitch-hiking between L.A. and San Francisco.

GREAT! SOCIETY"

DARBY SLICK- LEAD GUITAR
DAVID MINER- 2° GUITAR-VOCAL
GRACE SLICK - GUITAR-VOCAL
BARD DUPONT- HARMONICA BASS
JERRY SLICK- ELECTRIC PERCUSSION

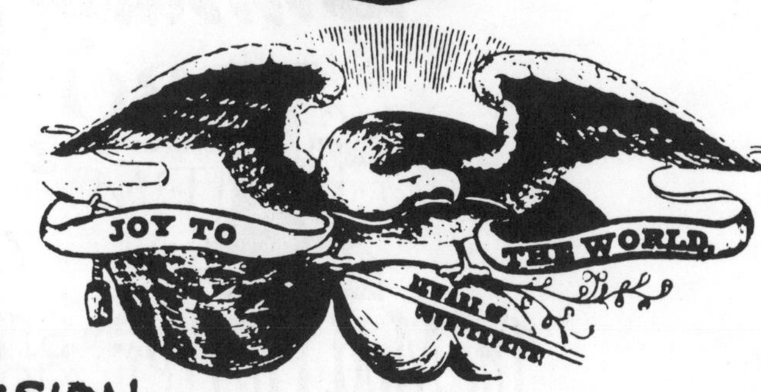

TMC - Mar.

The MOD HATTER
is using its
GRAND OPENING
as an excuse TO Present The
GREAT SOCIETY
OH?
mmmm
& INTERMISSION GROUPS
DANCING!
PLUS FREE
Pepsi! Jewelry!
BALLOONS!
(including expanding consciousness rings that fit any finger & magically turn green!
M. H. LOVES YOU
ALSO GIANT DRAWING for excruciatingly gorgeous MOD OUTFITS
HE WHO IS GEMINI IS IN ORBIT
Sunday June 26
1:30 P.M. to 6:00 P.M.
M. H. LOVES YOU
M. H. LOVES YOU
The Mod Hatter
STRAWBERRY TOWN & COUNTRY VILLAGE
MILL VALLEY

4

Early Dog Days

The thing was starting to happen. Critical mass. More, and more people were thinking the same way. There was even safety of a sort in these growing numbers. The dress code was ostensibly free; pick a costume, any costume, but not "straight clothes", that is, what had been, normal clothes of the period.

A friend of mine, Tom, was one of the most creative original and bizarre artists I knew. He was from Palo Alto, but I had met him through Leslie who had no direct Palo Alto connections. He worked in strange little sculptures, some of which had moving parts. Really, his was mixed media, because he also painted and incorporated painting in his sculptures in ways which I had never seen. He, almost alone of the people I knew, refused to change his clothing style. "I don't need to wear a costume to show I'm hip," he told me one day. "I don't want to be part of the new conformity, the old conformity's good enough for me." I had heard straight people question our individuality, but coming from Tom, it had more impact on me. Like Steve Martin, I thought, "Gee, maybe he's right.....naaaaaaaaah." I abandoned myself happily to the group.

We stopped being college students, and became pirates, or renaissance jugglers, or almost anything. Cowboy, not drugstore-shiny but nineteenth century black, was popular, as was anything that looked authentically Native American. The clothes of all foreign countries were fair game. It felt so liberating, but, above all, it was fun. Why should people in movies get to wear all the good clothes? I remember thinking that my choices were very original. At first, I wore shirts with what were called Edwardian, that is big, collars, a sports-jacket (preferably British), black jeans and Beatle boots. Then, I switched to brown suede boots, tight green jeans, and a horizontally striped black and yellow knit shirt. This was a sort of Robin Hood outfit. It felt to me, and I'm sure I wasn't alone, that we were becoming free. We were starting a new society. Now, I see that we were actually trying to escape from our own society, and God it seemed worth escaping from! So much of television and the movies had degenerated into formula settings. Here was the part where you were supposed to laugh, but who did, really? We were motivated by equal parts of boredom and fear. I don't think I knew anyone under that often cited age of 30 who thought that the world, or at least our advanced civilization, would survive for more than a few, or 10, years. It seemed impossible that so many atomic weapons could exist without someone using them. Human nature, which has some wonderful aspects, has, also, enough darkness to be scary when you add vast power into the formula. What will a generation do if it thinks that life holds no good promise? Party. It felt so good to walk around on the streets of San Francisco seeing all of the people who were committed to the new world. Long hair and clothing styles made the recognition factor just shoot across streets in instant communication. A feeling of family was coming into being that felt like it had never existed anywhere before. The closest analogy might be a tribe (my, what an original thought!) or a commune. Size was probably one of the most crucial factors. There had to be enough so that the group had substance, but, if the movement grew too large, individual responsibility would be lost, and people who didn't share the philosophy, but only the clothes, would wreck things. This is, in fact, what happened in 1967, when many who had been first on the scene declared, "Hippie Is Dead". But for a while, it was glorious.

By the fall of sixty six, the thing was getting big enough to need some outlets. These formed naturally in the community. The original Family Dog people lived in a Victorian house on Pine Street, in San Francisco, and, from there, they planned various activities. One of the first public ones, was a dance. They rented the Longshoreman's Hall, and began looking for bands who would embody the new sensibility. I don't remember if they heard about us, or we heard about them, but we arranged for them to come listen to us at Jerry and Grace's Larkspur house.

The sky was deep blue, the kind of blue that announces Fall even when the days are still hot. The leaves hung on the trees, ready to drop with the slightest breeze. I was nervous about the audition. We knew the songs; we had learned the shit out of the songs, the problem was that we didn't know how to play. We also didn't know how to rehearse. At rehearsals, we would start a song, and, every few beats, someone would stop it, and say to someone, "Don't play that, there." Or, "Play like this, here." We wouldn't be warmed up, or smooth and in the groove, or anything, and we'd be criticizing each other for not playing the parts competently. Each song had become a test with a million check points that each person had to hit correctly, in order for us to acknowledge that, yeh, that had been a pretty good run through.

I was sitting on the front steps, just finishing up a joint, and the universe was pulsing to the heart beat in my head, when the car pulled up. Out stepped Luria and Ellen, smiling and walking animatedly, with verve. They were the first hippie entrepreneurs, and they seemed excited about putting their new plans into practice. In some way, they were mother to a lot of what would follow, even perhaps, the Silicon Valley and people such as Steve Jobs.

I think that they, also, had just smoked a joint. Our recognition of each other as fellow whatevers was instant. Dogs sniffing. We went inside, and Grace made peppermint tea for us all. We talked of many things, quickly, again establishing the recognition signals. The front door was standing open, because the day was hot, but in deference to the police, we closed it before we began to play. I felt awkward, as I put on my guitar, intimidated to be playing for adult strangers; until that time, our only audience had been the local teenagers, who had stood outside listening to us with one ear while they talked. There were nowhere near as many bands in those days as there are now. People didn't much go into it thinking that they could become rich that way; the music business wasn't the giant industry that it would become. The local kids knew, and I think liked, us. But here were sophisticated adults whose sole mission at the moment, was to judge us. I was scared.

Tuning a guitar while stoned is an interesting proposition. Your ear seems, at once, too good, and then again, not good enough. The string sounds too sharp, or maybe, way too flat, all at the same time. It is quite possible to chase a string's tuning up and down, up and down, for an hour or so. And then, there are the other five strings, all of which must be tuned correctly to that first string. I have seen stoned people break strings chasing tuning, and I have seen them break guitars, in frustration. Since this was a live performance, rather than a taping, I limited myself to a few minutes of tuning, as did the others. Then, we began to play; what you hear is what you get. The Dog people said it was wonderful, and who am I to argue? For the last ten years or so, I'm writing this in 1991, musicians have been able to use cheap, electronic tuners, and this has made a world of difference. One of the prime characteristics of the San Francisco sound, was it's out-of-tuneness. If the slight variation in pitch between one instrument and another in classical music is called warmth, San Francisco music was really hot!

I don't think that the Dog people were very concerned with the quality of our music; they wanted to see if we were of the same ethos as they. Evidently, they decided that we were, because they enthusiastically agreed to hire us. We would be on the bill with the Jefferson Airplane, the Charlatans, and two
other bands that have essentially been forgotten: the Family Tree, and, I think, Captain Marvel.

The Charlatans were friends of mine. Jerry, Grace and I, used to visit them at their band house in the Haight-Ashbury. Mike Wilhelm was playing a Fender Jaguar guitar with them, and it was the nicest guitar I had ever seen. Whenever I'd drop by, I'd ask him to let me play it, because it was like a sports car compared to mine. I didn't necessarily like the sound better, but, next to Mike's, mine felt like it had been chopped out of a tree with a hatchet.

It was a Friday night in November of '66. Jerry and Grace and I were on our way to visit a friend, and we stopped by the Charlatan's Haight-Ashbury house. We knocked on the door, and George opened it, smiled from ear to ear, and invited us in. Walking up the front steps, we had heard electric guitar music. Now, inside, it was fairly loud. Mike was sitting on the floor in the living room stroking his Jaguar. He was using only his fingers, no pick. He was singing "Codeine". His singing was fine, but what moved me was the way he played the guitar, bringing subtle vibrato even to the chord notes. Grace sat shaking her head slowly from side to side with her eyes closed in appreciation of Mike's music.

When he finished, he said, "Go ahead, you know you want to." as he handed me the guitar. I did want to, but I felt intimidated playing solo guitar for other guitar players. I had only really developed a single note lead style that needed backing parts. Nonetheless, I took his guitar, and started playing blues licks with little chromatic ornaments vaguely similar to those in Indian music. Almost instantly, I forgot about the others in the room, and got into the world of music. After some time, I stopped playing and handed him back the guitar. "Cool." he said, receiving it and launching into a Stones song.

We had a lot of mutual friends, and often ended up at the same parties. These parties seemed enormously fun at the time: New records, drugs and alcohol, sexual tensions (and releases). The Charlatans' leader, George Hunter, had been a friend for a few years before any of us put bands together.

George assembled his group, and got them a job playing all summer, the summer of '65, in Virginia City. I think the place was called the Red Dog Saloon. He made a beautiful poster for the gig, and, although it was also to be seen in Virginia City, he plastered San Francisco with it. In this way, he accomplished several good things. The band opened out of town, and so was able to get it's chops together unreviewed. Quite a few hippies drove up to see them, and the context couldn't have been more perfect for their looks and music; they came across as sort of Victorian-cowboy-Rolling Stones.

I drove up with my girl friend Leslie, and we spent a couple of days with them. It was hot as we arrived on that Friday afternoon. The main street looked old-West and tourist-haven at the same time. Above the Red Dog Saloon, on the second floor, Mike Ferguson (the group's piano player) was standing with his upper body sticking out of the open window. He called to us as we got out of the car, "Hey Darby, what's happening?" This question didn't call for an actual answer; "Hey, man." was all I said. We went up to their rooms, and listened as they, excited but ever cool, told us of their summer. They had each ordered custom-made pistols at the local gunsmith's shop. The local sheriff was treating them with respect, and their gig was going well (all of these things would sour over the summer). They showed us around town, and introduced us to some hip local people who invited us to stay with them for the weekend. The heat was still oppressive, and we all went to a local swimming-hole, where we lay around on the big smooth hot rocks, smoking joints and swimming occasionally, to cool off.

"Jesus Christ, it's hot." I said. Just as marijuana intensifies hunger, so it does heat and cold, sex and loneliness.

"Yeh, and at night, it's colder than a motherfucker," said Mike Ferguson, "but you should see the stars, man."

But we had no out of doors, communing with the Cosmos experience that night. Instead, we went to hear them play, and I really liked it. They all wore black, and, somehow, they managed to appear, at once, good-timey and sinister. George played auto-harp on some songs, and that, with the other instruments, gave them a shimmering zingy high quality. On other songs, George played tambourine, and he used to wear a knee pad pulled up high on the thigh under his pants, to protect himself from the tambourine; nonetheless, I think he managed to beat himself up pretty good with it in the course of an evening. Dan Hicks played drums with them, and his style, simple and direct but with almost Spike Jones overtones, perfectly suited their mood. The Charlatans had gone to Virginia City with their image substantially formed already, but, I think, during the course of the summer, they learned how to act the part, as well as look it.

When they returned to San Francisco, their reputations were made. They had the advantage of being locals as well as touring pros. Not only were they good friends with, and almost part of, the Family Dog, but they had worked as much in that summer, as most of us would in the next year.

There were few chances for a hippie group to play five nights a week, and I don't think many of us would have, even if the opportunity had been there; it's hard to create new songs and band arrangements while working that steadily. Most of us had not settled into a set list and a style at this point, so we needed lots of rehearsals to get our acts together.

The Jefferson Airplane had a vibe of success right from the start. I don't know if it was an inner self-confidence that they projected, or whether it was based on essentially external facts, such as having money or management and other factors like those. To me, they seemed snobbish. My reaction was, "What makes these guys think they're such hot shit?" My attitude was unfortunate, especially as I should have known better; I had, myself, been regarded with suspicion and occasionally, derision, by the kids I grew up with because I aspired to loftier things, art for example, than they considered to be normal and desirable. Perhaps the Airplane people, particularly Marty and Paul, were early leaders of the self-esteem movement.

The original Airplane was far more folk oriented than the one that became famous. Their bass player played a stand-up bass, and acoustic guitar featured prominently in their sound. They were, exactly, folk-rock. They were also very show-biz. They smiled a lot, and projected a clean-cut image. Marty used, sometimes, to drop down on one knee, while singing a ballad. Their vocal harmonies were powerful, and there's no doubt that, overall, they were the best singing band of the new San Francisco groups. Their song "It's No Secret" was a favorite of mine, and it was extremely popular. I could see their obvious commercial appeal, and this was the very thing I held against them. Perhaps I was not alone, and they sensed this, because when they became famous, their stance was blatantly anti-commercial.

It is interesting to me, that I don't remember much about our music, or the experience of making our music at the Great Society's first two shows: the Coffee Gallery, and this first Family Dog concert. I do remember that the Coffee Gallery gig really did help, in that, when our band started to sound odd to us, we knew to just keep playing and not worry about it very much. Getting used to the acoustics, or sound, of each new place was a big part of the challenge of live performance.

The Family Dog concert was named, " A Tribute to Dr. Strange", after the comic book of the same name. The overwhelming part of the experience, for me, and I think, virtually for everyone who attended, was the certainty of the birth of a scene. We, the collective we, had arrived, and there were so many of us, and we were weird, and interesting, and lovable. The large round concrete building was full. The excitement was intense, and vibrant. The atmosphere was completely different than at the commercial concerts put on by Big Daddy Tom Donahue at the Cow Palace. This was not only a party, it was our party, by and for the people. The fact that money was involved was very unimportant. Few of us were married, and few had kids; we weren't saving up for braces for their teeth, nor were we trying to establish family empires to stretch through time. Oh, we wanted to get paid. We wanted money for rent, food, drugs (drugs were cheap then), gas and car repair, and a few other small expenses. One thousand dollars a month could easily support a whole band and the attendant families.

The title of the show beautifully set the mood. Only freaks, as we lovingly called ourselves, would want to attend something called, " A Tribute to Dr. Strange". Many of us used to smoke dope and read those comic books. I don't know if their authors and illustrators used drugs, but, at the time, we all thought so. The comic characters seemed always to be warping in and out of strange mental worlds, and the illustrations looked psychedelic.

As the next year proceeded, there came to be many people that I recognized at these shows. Some adopted a particular face-painting, or costume, or both, and became easily recognizable. Some I just saw every week or so, and got to know on sight. Many I never spoke with, but I felt that I knew them and they, me. Things happened that I think of as happening in small towns, or in time of war; if a hippie's car broke down, another hippie would stop to help. Small courtesies were commonplace, and even large amounts of money, and other resources, such as time and land, were often shared. The joy wasn't in the costumes we wore, per say, but in the community that we built with them. It was as if we established a new race, and ourselves as members of it.

There were, at first, almost no imitators, or interlopers, because word hadn't gotten out. This was probably never truer than at the first Family Dog show. If you're not a philatelist, you don't tend to consider infiltrating a meeting of those who are, so that you can adopt their mannerisms and clothing, and party with them. We were with our own for the first time, and we were ecstatic, and optimistically curious about the short-term future, and, for one night, we forgot that the world would soon end.

5

Jammin' With Garcia

The Mission District on a Friday evening has always been an exciting place. The lights of the beer signs blink and spin, shooting neon sparks out into the darkening sky. People have just gotten paid, and no matter how oppressing their lives might feel to them, in fact because of the oppression, they are now ready for fun, and fuck those bills, we'll worry about them tomorrow. The women dress and make-up for action, and the men have also done their homework. Radios snake Latin rhythms. Cars stop in mid-street, while friends and would-be lovers communicate with soul projection, gestures and words. The psychic pace is hectic, and mostly joyful; there is little trouble this early in the evening. Trouble will come later, when too much alcohol will bring interior frustration to the surface.

The Mission still had lofts, in the 60's. Sometimes huge lofts would be partitioned into rooms, and the rooms would be rented by artists. Sometimes, they would be left undivided and used as rehearsal halls.

Jerry and Grace and I were going to one of these large lofts now, to a party, we were told, a jam; non-band people would be asked to donate money to something, I think, the Mime Troupe.

We drove through crowds of locals who knew and cared nothing about the loft happenings. Our car stopped repeatedly in the traffic, which was always a sort of mini Mardi Gras. There was seldom only one loud radio playing, although this was mercifully before the boom-box's stomach pounding bass. The sound world was a complex and changing mixture of musics, car horns, shouts, talking and laughter, with the obligatory police siren functioning as the lemon rind on the side of the cocktail.

I was excited, inhaling the vibe, along with the smoke from the joint Jerry had just handed me. People and music, dope and celebrity, life was happening. Our local status was such that we were welcomed and helped, given free drugs, invited in, you name it, wherever we went. I was completely unconscious of the way celebrity stroked my ego, and I took it as my birthright, but it, along with the mild paranoia that marijuana inclined me towards, was starting to make me uncomfortable with non-band people; I was starting to walk quickly through a hall or club, and seek, immediately, the musician's room. Even there, I was usually tense, because being there involved talking with musicians from other bands, and managers, photographers, all of the people in the, what was then, little business. Everyone was friendly, but I was tense.

"What's supposed to be happening tonight?" I asked Jerry, who was driving with his usual brake and gas, whiplash technique.

"Shit, I don't know," he said, "they just said come by, if we want, and jam. I don't think anything's really been planned."

"Fuck that," said Grace.

"You could just sing the blues, or something." I said.

"I don't know how to sing the blues," she said.

"What about that Dylan song we've been working on, Outlaw Blues?" I asked.

Grace turned and looked at me with a frowning mouth and big eyes. Her hostility seemed directed as much at herself as at me.

"Shit man," she said, "I don't want to sing with those other guys. I don't know what the fuck they're going to do next, or even when they're going to change chords."

"Just see how it goes," said Jerry, "maybe you'll feel like it at the time."

As we approached the address, we saw the crowd. There were about 50 people talking on the street, and another 50 or so around the doorway making a serious effort to get inside. There were no parking spaces anywhere near, so we continued on in the direction of Potrero Hill for about three blocks, and finally parked the car across the driveway of a cement company that was closed for the night.

Walking back in cold night air that was thick with the smell of roasting coffee from the nearby M.J.B. plant, I shoved my left hand deep in my jeans' pocket, balled my fist, and hunched my shoulders; my right arm, I held tight to my side, as I clutched the handle of my guitar case in cold fingers. Some geese flew across the face of the moon, heading south. I kicked at pieces of gravel left by the cement trucks. We walked quickly, Grace drinking her champagne from a small bottle "hidden" in a brown paper bag.

"I wish I'd brought my kick pedal," said Jerry, "I don't mind playing someone else's drums, but I hate like shit to play a different pedal. It's real hard to a get a groove going when the throw's all different.

"Fuck it," I said, "fuck 'em if they can't take a joke."

As we approached the building, people recognized us, and said hi, and things like that. A young man with jet black hair and blazing blue eyes said, "Take me in with you." to which Grace smiled and laughed in a friendly way. We excused ourselves as we wormed through the crowd on the stairs, and at the top, we were virtually grabbed by the door guard, and pulled inside. The large, hall-sized room was totally packed, standing room only, and in such a tightly packed room, no one would have dared to sit down, even around the edges.

Again, we wormed our way through the crowd towards the three or four foot high stage at the south-west corner of the room. Music filled the air, and I could see Jerry Garcia, and hear his bright, folky, funky, guitar melodies. I felt a little nervous, but intensely happy.

The stage had a back portion to it, behind the amplifiers, though it wasn't an actual separated backstage area; there was no curtain. Someone, I think it was either Danny Rifkin or Rock Scully, was functioning as stage manager in the loose way that the situation called for, just talking to the musicians who might want to jam, and setting it up. My brother and I said, sure we'd love to play, but Grace stuck to her reticence; though improvisation is one of her strongest gifts, she seems to prefer to employ it in the context of known musicians playing known songs. The stage manager said, "Jerry (Garcia) is really hot tonight. He wants to just play and play. Why don't you join him and see what you all can get going?" Bill Kreutzmann was playing drums, and I think Peter Albin was playing bass. Many people cheered when I walked out next to where Jerry Garcia was standing, further inflating my already swollen ego. This scene was just too cool, and I knew it. My brother Jerry joined Bill on a second set of drums, and we all started to jam the blues, almost the only music we could launch into with no more discussion than, "It's in `A'." Most of the time, for the next forty five minutes or so, Garcia and I took turns playing solos for a few chorus' each, just passing it back and forth like a joint. When he played lead, I put my head down and towards the left, almost like a violinist, and dug into the rhythm. I have always loved playing rhythm guitar, so it was a great pleasure to back him up in that way. Harmonically, I played simple chords, but tried to make powerful and unusual rhythm statements. When I played lead, he smiled and smiled his beautiful smile, even laughing occasionally when I played some particularly dissonant phrase; one of my main goals in music, was to break it open and play something really weird that had never been played before, and I was willing to jump off the cliff in order to, hopefully, fly. I was a great admirer of Ornette Coleman, and I wanted my melodies to be quirky like his, but with my own stamp. Few of my attempts to get "outside" made it to disk, but the solo on the Great Society version of "White Rabbit" (Columbia Records) contains examples of this.

Garcia and I played more to each other than to the crowd, communicating with our guitars at least as directly as people ever do with words, and folks loved it; everyone can tell when something real is happening, and though our playing contained elements of show-boating, all was done with humor and love. My brother and Bill similarly "talked" to each other and to us, and I could see joy on both their faces. The bass thundered with more bottom than you usually hear nowadays, and the whole thing just seemed to work. When music is really happening, it creates a new world, or even a new universe. Time, in the normal sense, seems to disappear, and the "now" opens up and becomes all pervasive. Notes, riffs, chords, and rhythms become elements that make up the world, and there is acceptance, and even bliss, associated with their position; when I look at a beach, I never say, "This is great, but that piece of driftwood should be a little to the left." Another thing that happens, from the musician's perspective, is that the music seems to play itself. I have marvelled at what I was playing right as I played it, and have even been so detached from it, that I was able to carry on a conversation with someone and simultaneously play far better than I normally do. This was one of those nights: no effort, only ease and a whole range of emotions coming through the music.

Gradually, each of our solos became shorter as we threw phrases back and forth to each other. The mood was building, the intensity increasing. I would "ask" a musical "question", and he would "answer" it. Occasional bits of one-upmanship were not vicious; neither of us tried for a knockout blow, nor even to inflict damage. There was magic in the room that night, and though I have played in many jam sessions through the years, that is the one I remember with the most love, the most respect. When it built to its huge crescendo, and then was over, I felt like a different person than when I started; inner, soul, values became more important, and outer, nervous matters, less. I was left with a conviction that Jerry Garcia is a man of great spirit.

Garcia...

His hair was fuzzy and his crooked smile curved up higher on one side. His eyes had sparkles that drugs couldn't extinguish. His commitment to the guitar was big, maybe not total like Jimi's, but big. Of course, I had never heard of Jimi then. Parapsychotics grew out of his ears, and glands hung hugely down, dripping excesses. His voice was soft, and croaked somewhat, perfectly matching the ironic content it purveyed. His sideburns threatened his large nose. The rabbit seemed ever willing to pop up out of his stovepipe hat, and a little thing like changing one's seat on the train mustn't be allowed to throw one, but somehow it always does, but not him. The barometer was dropping into the sound arena out of the visible light spectrum. How to know what effect not taking drugs would have had on any of us? I hate to blanket a generation, but I can't recall anyone deciding not to take drugs. I remember people refusing specific drugs on specific occasions, most

> often unknown drugs like, "Here, take this orange and blue one." "What is it?" "Fuck, I don't know." Sometimes, "Okay", sometimes, "Naaah", but everyone I knew took drugs. Frank Zappa wasn't here (it can't happen here). This was our Vietnam, the Battle of the Brain Cells, and drugs were the weapons, the transport ships, the airplanes, and people were the weapons too. We scraped each other with our knives flat, removing flesh in flakes and chunks, not killing, but only partially dismembering. "Do I contradict myself? Very well, then, I contradict myself." Peace and love.

Some say move on, and we do, what choice have we, but it moves on with us, living still, as history does in Faulkner's south, and maybe everywhere else. The bravery that is required of one, dumped onto this backwater planet with no guarantees, and amidst so much pain! Easier to shut it out, as in Star Trek with the billions of souls marching by, outside of Captain Kirk's luxury window.

6

The Very First Fillmore Show

Jerry's old brown Falcon station wagon was missing a little, as we rode over the Golden Gate Bridge into San Francisco. He drove, Grace sat in the middle, and I sat on the right, what we used to call shotgun. Sitting this close to Grace still made me uncomfortable, that is, mildly aroused, so I held on to the arm rest and tried not to bounce into her as we went over bumps and around corners. She appeared, possibly without artifice, not to notice my discomfort; I think that sometimes she enjoyed it. We were all a little nervous, but in a different way, perhaps, than we would be in the future.

We were on our way to the Fillmore Auditorium to play a concert that was being put on by Bill Graham. He was, as we were, nobody. The Fillmore was nothing special, just another hall about town. This was the first Bill Graham Fillmore Auditorium show. It was a benefit for the San Francisco Mime Troupe, and I liked them a lot. They were not mimes in the sense of silent actors; they put on humorously left-wing plays, often in parks, for free, and they were loved and appreciated by most who saw them. In the days before Reagan, the right had almost no credibility in San Francisco, and businessmen (there were damn few women) seemed almost embarrassed by their own commerce. Whenever they could, they changed out of their business suits, and often pretended to be in the "looser" walks of life.

Old time Communists and labor leaders abounded, as did scholars, teachers, artists, and assorted glamorous riffraff. A Sunday in Golden Gate Park with an audience of all ages relaxing and enjoying the Mime Troupe, was a very pleasant day. Sometimes, their costumes suggested Shakespeare's England, and the green lawns and trees of the park heightened the renaissance feeling. They have usually been in financial trouble, and when Bill Graham took over as their business manager, they were in desperate need.

After we had pulled up to the front door of the hall, Jerry and Grace went in to announce our arrival, and ask about a musician's load-in, and I stayed with the car to guard the stuff. I lit a Pall Mall, and leaned up against the car, looking cool. I often went to the Fillmore district, a mostly black area in those days, to visit friends and eat barbecue, and sweet potato pie. There was little racial tension and little robbery. Many black people seemed somewhat bemused to see the hippie hairstyles and clothes, although, there were, of course, many black hippies. This bemusement sometimes turned into amusement, but never, that I'm aware of, into hostility.

Jerry and Grace came out, and the three of us began to carry the equipment up the short flight of stairs, through the old-cigarette smelling foyer, across the boomy auditorium and up to the chest-high stage. We tried to stagger our trips, so that one person stayed in view of the car, and I've continued this simple precaution through the years. Jerry had disassembled his drums for travel, and it was easy to pinch a finger in the collapsed, metal highhat parts, so I carried it carefully; would that I had been as cautious in all areas of health and safety! I felt big-time, carrying in the stuff, and knowing that later we would be, I hoped, playing for a large crowd. I know that Jerry and Grace felt this too, for I could see the corners of their mouths turn up repeatedly in doyish smiles, and our conversation became banter. Today, when I see a young band setting up, I recognize the look on their faces and the sound in their voices. It sort of communicates, "God damn, this is really happening and it's pretty fucking alright!"

I was just beginning to learn how dirty stages are. Performers often look glamorous from the audience, and it is easy to think that their environment must be glamorous also. The floor is usually carpeted in some awful stuff, dirty, and with marks and debris from years of performances.

Some technician was busy setting up microphones. These mikes were for the singers, only. Even though the Fillmore is a small hall, now, each instrument would be miked and the drums would have at least three mikes. Then, we didn't know any better. I say that the Fillmore is a small hall, and it is, but, in those days, it seemed huge to us. A few years ago, Bill Graham had a 20th reunion party there, and word went out to most who had populated the Fillmore, onstage, and off. It was wonderful being with those people, many of whose faces were still familiar, but with whom I have never spoken, either at all, or, at least, more than casually. The most repeated comment was," It's so small."

We set up our equipment on stage, and did a sound check. The big, empty-box hall, which had received not one iota of acoustic planning, echoed like an early rockabilly record. The slap-back was almost as loud as the original sound, making it difficult to play. "Don't worry," we were told, "when it fills up, the people will absorb a lot of sound."

We pushed our equipment to the back of the stage, to make room for the next band, and left to go eat. Grace used to like to go to an awful place on Van Ness, called the Doggy Diner. The place was all white plastic, with a few black plastic accents. The light was harsh strong florescent. Huge rounded doorways stood constantly open to the weather. The food was hot dogs and chili, and was truly terrible. I don't know why Grace liked it. I drank a coke, because I couldn't stand the food. The three of us chain smoked; Luckys for Jerry, Pall Malls for me, and some kind of menthol filters for Grace. She shoved the butt of one into the remains of her chilidog on its little yellow paper boat (or was it a kennel?), and we walked out of the restaurant, whose cold air was sharply broken by beams from heat lamps. Grace had on a dirty beige trenchcoat, which she wore almost daily at the time. Sometimes she didn't wear clothes under it, but today, she was dressed in a short black skirt, boots, and a white blouse; this was one of her favorite outfits, or, at least, she wore it a lot. She laughed often, but she seemed, under her bravado, to be scared shit-less.

We stopped at a corner store on the way back, and bought some supplies: champagne, beer, cigarettes. My throat hurt from the chain smoking, but I couldn't slow down. The Coffee Gallery had been sort of a lark, and the first Family Dog show had been a revelation. What would tonight be?

We parked on the street, there was no special parking and no one to help, and walked with exaggerated slowness towards the hall, wanting to look cool, to each other as much as to any one else. My feet were soaking wet with sweat in my old suede boots, and the cold wind went right through my thin clothes. I had that almost-a-headache I would come to know so well.

Arriving back at the hall, we told the agreeable rent-a-cop that we were performing, there were no passes of any kind, things just weren't that organized yet, and he let us in. We walked to the musician's room, which was up a flight of stairs to the left of the stage. We were laughing nervously and horsing around with each other. I had complete confidence in our material, at least that which was written by Grace. If she had shit in her hand and handed it to me, I would have said, "Oh what an inspired creation." What I still lacked confidence in, was our ability to play the material convincingly. Occasionally, when we practiced, things got so fucked-up, that we actually ground to a halt. We had had to make a rule; no matter what happens, don't stop playing until the song is over. I've seen other young bands do this, and it's always a kick (for the non-participants); it's like watching a robot become tangled in it's own limbs.

The first couple of bands played, and we waited our turn, as the house filled up. Someone had warned us that the rent-a-cops would turn us in if they caught us smoking dope, so we didn't, we only drank. At last it was time. We hurriedly shoved our equipment to the front of the pile, and began to play. The slap-back was just as bad as it had been in the afternoon, and we all played louder, trying to overpower it with volume; for Jerry, that meant hitting his drums harder than he had ever hit them. Of course, this tactic doesn't work, but it does explain the look of consternation on Jerry's face when, after the first song, I walked over to him and said, "would you mind playing a little louder?" He had beat the shit out of his arms on the first song, and was wondering where he would get the strength to play the next song, let alone the rest of the set.

Jerry's part on the second song involved complex interplay between the high hat, kick, and snare. The part was so complicated that he had to count his way into it, and give it his full concentration, just to keep it going. Of course, no one had told Bill Graham this, and, a few moments into the song, he walked over to Jerry, and began to discuss something, perhaps future bookings, with him. Jerry could only make his eyes very large, and continue playing with a sort of, "Oh, Shit" look on his face. At some point, Bill must have realized that if he wanted any response, he was going to have to talk to Jerry later.

Grace really fired her performance at the audience. Right from the start, she would get a little drunk, and use that part of her in-your-face personality to virtually attack the audience. It worked! At the time, there were few female performers who came on really aggressively, and there were none on the local scene (this was before Janis hit town). Grace was a lot more like Sophie Tucker or Ethel Merman than she was like Marianne Faithfull or Petula Clark. She swore like a truck driver, unusual in 1965, and swaggered and posed onstage in ways that had been, hitherto, masculine, but she was not masculine in her looks at all. People often described her as a gutsy broad. Her fears and self-doubts were completely hidden by her slightly drunken bravado, and she appeared to be the most confident performer who had ever come down the pike. Audiences loved this in her; it was more than reassuring. Rather than," I'm okay, you're okay", it was, "everything's fucking wonderful". She didn't just leap around in high-energy abandonment; she would stand very still, singing into the microphone she held up to her mouth, and then she would run suddenly to the edge of the stage and bend forward to deliver the next phrase right at some particular person. Her unpredictability made it hard not to watch her.

She did many things to establish contact with the audience. She would point to someone and say, "Hey, I like your hat". A simple statement like that really said many things: that she was sure enough of herself to know what she liked and didn't like (and would tell you about it), that she wasn't just doing some produced-to-death act, that we were all here and now, and that, to some degree at least, we were all in this show together.

To me, each of the San francisco bands was magic, and the magic was different in each band. Ours came largely from Grace's personality, and from our desire to experiment and our love of many of the world's musics.

We lifted and or adapted, parts from Miles Davis records (Sketches of Spain), Ravi Shankar records, and many other sources. When we did a cover tune, we tried to make it sound very different from the original. We'd say, "Lets mix some of this with some of that, and see how it sounds." Often, the combination would suggest alterations in the original components, and we'd have something interesting enough to keep.

Our view of Rock and Roll was that it should be like found art and collages, a reshuffling of existing elements. In this show, the Second Mime Troupe Benefit, we were mixing pretty simple ideas and riffs, but later, when Peter Van Gelder replaced Bard du Pont on bass, our brews became stranger; we changed between exotic time signatures for various sections, mixed the sounds of jazz with rock and roll, and tried everything we could think of to develop polyrhythms.

The playbill of this show was very typical of what would be Bill Graham's shows; there was a group called the Gentleman's Band which was a local Black group, a couple of rock and roll bands, a jazz group, in this case John Handy. The rock and roll groups, or psychedelic if you will, were the Mystery Trend, the Great Society, and the Jefferson Airplane. Bill Graham seemed to like this format, it worked for him , and he stuck with it for a long time. He would honor a local group, and the community, by hiring a Black group; usually they were the opening act, and a lot of the white kids, who were the predominant attenders, didn't pay them much attention. The jazz group was sort of for Bill's benefit in a way. He liked jazz, and sometimes he would use a latin group because he also loved that music. He really believed in educating his clientele; he thought that, jazz being a higher art form, introducing the kids to it would be good for them and good for jazz. And of course the rock and roll bands, the local psychedelic, and later the imported bands, were the bread and butter. They would be the draw, the main part of the show.

At this show, and at all the shows I know about afterwards, Bill Graham was jumping around like a nut; he was everywhere at once, and doing every job that needed to be done. He wasn't really stopping his people from doing their jobs, he wasn't really interfering in that sense, but he was sure running in to take up any slack he found anywhere. I remember a friend telling me that when Bob Dylan brought his new electric band to town, Bill sold my friend popcorn at intermission, an example of how ubiquitous Bill was, and I believe, still is.

Ron Nagle had put together a band called the Mystery Trend. He was a friend of Jerry and Grace's and mine, and Ron's philosophy was very similar, in the art sense, to ours; he would stick various elements together, some of which went together more harmoniously than others, as we did. We were a pretty natural double bill, and we worked together quite a few times in these early days. Once, we even played with them on a show they put together themselves. I liked the Mystery Trend a lot, because of their just blatant experimentalism, their willingness to try things that were truly weird, and that was something that I admired, and I think I admire it as much today. It just seems that there are so many people in music, including myself sometimes, playing it safe, that it's really great to see somebody who's willing to break out and try to create something new, and especially something that's new to them; that's the part that's really hard to come by. Some people have concepts that are new to them and they develop them privately, and bring them out to us, and they're new to us, but if someone can be tricking themselves, that's when I like it best, and that's something that I used to try to do a lot. I would just jump to some note and trip out from the sound that came out and try to go from there, and Ron was doing that a lot compositionally and individuals were doing that in his group, so I liked them.

John Handy was a very sweet man, and his music showed it. The sound that comes from his horn is round and true, and his blues knowledge infuses everything he plays with organic authority. Being on the bill with him this night, I wasn't really able to listen to him, so I don't know how this particular outing was for him, though he seemed totally ecstatic after his set as he dabbed the sweat from his round forehead with the handkerchief which he had just removed from the pocket of his immaculate, grey, sharkskin suit. Within a few weeks of this performance, I went to hear him play on Fillmore Street, at the Both\And, I think, and I loved his playing. I've heard him many times through the years, in fact for a while, he and Ali Akbar Khan played tasty and adventuresome duets together, and I've continued to love his playing, as well as his genuine beauty of character.

The audience at this show was composed of the same types, and many of the same people, who had attended the first Family Dog show. These concert-dances were the first points on the straight line road to Hippiedom.

From here, it took Bill Graham about three weeks to mount his next Fillmore show, then two weeks for the next one, and then every week forever after, on into different venues and locations.

7

Big Daddy

Tom Donahue was a disk jockey at the most popular station in town. He began to promote shows at, what was then, the largest bay area arena, the Cow Palace (I think it was Paul Mc Cartney who would ask, "You want us to play at the what?", thereby causing us to actually notice the name of the place for the first time). Tom had a business associate, a fellow-jock named Bobby Mitchell, but as far as I could tell, Mitchell was largely a money man. Tom was living with a beautiful and highly intelligent young woman named Rachel. I think she started out as only a girlfriend, but soon, she and Tom were partners in every sense.

I missed the beginning of Tom's days as a record label owner, but by the time the Great Society auditioned for him at Mother's in early '66, he had built up a little stable of artists, and had an unknown, but extremely talented, producer, Sly Stone. Tom also had an agent-publicist named Carl Scott: I don't know how the money went, but they worked together. Tom's nickname was "Big Daddy", and he and Carl were both way overweight; together, they made quite a pair!

Tom's label was named Autumn Records, and with it he had several hits. The excellent singer and dancer Bobby Freeman, for example, scored with "C'Mon Let's Swim". Tom's group, the Beau Brummels, imitated the

British groups, and hit with "Laugh Laugh".

Tom saw the hippie thing happening, and he wanted to be part of it. He and Mitchell had just taken over a club on Broadway which they named Mother's. They decorated it with Pseudo-psychedelic paint, heavy on purple, orange ,and green, and put an ad in the Chronicle for auditions leading to club work and a record contract. We, and many others, responded. Many of Donahue's groups came just for the hell of it, and they, and the other auditioners, comprised the audience.

Waiting for our turn, we saw many polished groups, often they did choreographed dance steps, but most seemed boring and lacking in originality. When our turn came, we did a few songs in our inept, but adventurous, way, while the pros, I particularly remember the Mojo Men, sat howling with laughter. Tom and Sly, however, liked us, and we were obviously really part of the scene, rather than jaded top 40 musicians trying to glom on. Later, we became friends with the Mojo Men; it was easy to relate to their desire to make money to feed their families, and they related to our desire to do weird, new things.

We were asked to a local studio to make a quick, one-pass version of all of our songs preliminary to signing a contract. We agreed. It all seemed so easy. First big hippie rock show coming up? One audition and we get the job. Wanna make a record? One audition and we get a contract. Things were not always to be this easy.

We went to the recording studio and did quickie versions of our songs. Ray Andersen came and photographed the session. Donahue then reviewed the tape, and offered us a "standard", read not very good, contract, which we changed to give us total control of everything. The word in those days was that you wanted control of everything creative: album cover, song selection, arrangement, final mix, and mastering mother (the "mold" from which the actual records are made). Money mattered less to us, because, while money would be okay, we didn't want people to make us look like dorks (or Monkees!). We also didn't want to be hung up endlessly if the company just wasn't happening, so we put in a clause releasing us from the contract if product didn't come out within a specified time, I think it was six months or a year.

Tom introduced us to Carl Scott who was to book us, and to get articles written in teen magazines. The whole thing was set up for the old idea, as if Grace was to be the next Fabian. We complained, but, for a while, went along with filling out questionnaires asking what signs we were, what were our favorite foods and colors. It seemed that they would promote us, but, as what?

Tom got us a "rehearsal studio", a huge, empty, echoing chamber with ceiling, floor, and walls made entirely from thick cement. We could play one note and take a ten minute break waiting for it to die out. Ruling this out after one trial, we began rehearsing in Donahue's office, after hours. The office was good for us, because we got to meet a lot of people there regularly: Tom's protegee, Bob McClay, Jim Gavin, of the Gavin Report, on and on, including of course, all of Donahue's other groups.

We worked on our own songs, but I also remember learning three obscure Chuck Berry songs in that little office; Chuck had been a favorite of all of ours in high school. In moments of boredom, we began to pick up copies of Billboard Magazine that were lying around the office, and it began to dawn on us that music was a business not unlike shoe sales.

Donahue's producer was Sly Stone, a young disk jockey on the local R & B stations. Sly seemed to be able to play just about every instrument. I've heard him sound cool on guitar, bass, drums, organ and harmonica. Sly produced all of Donahue's acts: the Beau Brummels, the Mojo Men, the Vejtables, Bobby Freeman, George and Teddy. Naturally, Tom asked him to produce us. Perhaps in film, "producer" is a job title with specific responsibilities, but in music, it varies greatly. A record producer might do everything from picking the songs and playing all the instruments, to almost nothing. In the days when the hippie musicians insisted on being boss, company-hired producers often sat by uninvolved at sessions in moods of boredom mixed with quiet despair.

Our first take on Sly was, yeh, he's cool. He wanted to come to a practice, and start working with us. Fine, we said. At that first practice, we offered him a joint. He reluctantly smoked a little with us; he seemed somewhat afraid of drugs, and unused to them. He started making arrangement suggestions, and, one by one, we rejected them. Things were the way they were, we said, because we liked them that way. He became dejected and angry.

"What the fuck do you need with a producer if you're going to axe all my ideas?" he asked.

"Did we ask for a producer?" I asked.

"Maybe not, and you can bet your asses I didn't ask for you either." We all sat, silent, for several minutes. Then, Sly spoke, his voice heavy with resignation.

"Look, you guys do what you want, it don't make me no nevermind. I'll be cool with Donahue, and I'll come to the sessions and try to help you with some of the tricks of the studio okay?"

"Yeh, cool." I said.

Sly was exceedingly kind and wise beyond his years in his acceptance of our egocentric demands to do it our way. The result was, that we actually did take some of his advice in the studio, and he was able to help us some. If he had tried to force his ways on us, we would never have accepted, but would rather have preferred to leave the label. We were very afraid of losing whatever was unique about ourselves.

We started a run at Donahue's club, playing five sets a night, six nights a week, for what seemed eternity, but must have been a month or so. We had only two sets of material, so we did set one, set two, set one, set two, and lastly, a set of the "best" material from sets one and two. God pity you if you spent a whole evening with us! Our playing improved, and we became more used to performing during this time. Another advantage, was that we were motivated to write more material so that we wouldn't have to repeat so many songs.

I was living with Leslie. She was working at the post office, Rincon Annex, which, in those days, was a haven for hippies and various intellectuals. Leslie loved rock and roll, but grew, by her statements, jealous of the attention I was receiving. One night, I was home alone while she was working. I took some L.S.D., and waited for her. She didn't come home. From hints she had dropped, which I hadn't understood, but had registered in my memory, I knew that she wasn't injured, but was with someone else. At dawn, coming down from the drug, and miserable about our disintegrating relationship, I sat with my guitar and wrote:

When the truth is found to be lies
And all the joy within you dies,

Don't you want somebody to love?

Don't you need somebody to love

Wouldn't you love somebody to love,

you better find somebody to love.

The whole song came very quickly, words and music. I had no tape recorder, and didn't know how to write music notation, so I played it over and over for many hours, often sobbing as I tried to croak out the words. Finally, I went to sleep.

A few days later, Leslie called me, and we formally broke up. I felt many emotions: loss, sadness, hurt, optimism, joy, invincibility. I loved Leslie, and I loved the song: too many emotions. I drank, and took drugs, and moved on.

I remember walking into Mother's for an afternoon, pre-gig rehearsal.

"Hey, I've got a new song," I said, "you gotta hear it."

Jerry and Grace, Bard and David, flipped over it. Everyone around us who heard it said, that's a hit! There sure wasn't any doubt in my mind. We worked up an arrangement with Grace singing lead, David, harmony. I played two solos in different spots, the first, mellow-sounding and sad, the second, loud and angry, as the song built.

About three days later, Grace came into a similar rehearsal and said, " Wait 'till you hear my new song!" She walked over to her small keyboard, and started playing and singing:

One pill makes you larger,

One pill makes you small

The ones your mother gives you,

Don't do anything at all

She had always loved Lewis Carrol, Ravel's Bolero, and Miles Davis' Sketches of Spain, so she had written a song based on Alice in Wonderland, with a Spanish-sounding, building, music. It climaxed with her virtually screaming, "Feed your head!"

It was a knockout song, obviously a hit, and we were now ecstatic; we had stuff we thought of as art, that we were sure people would love. Nothing could stop us. That was an amazing week for me. I was so full of emotions, they were like physical presences pumping through my blood. I cried many times on stage, behind my wrap-around shades, often unable to tell

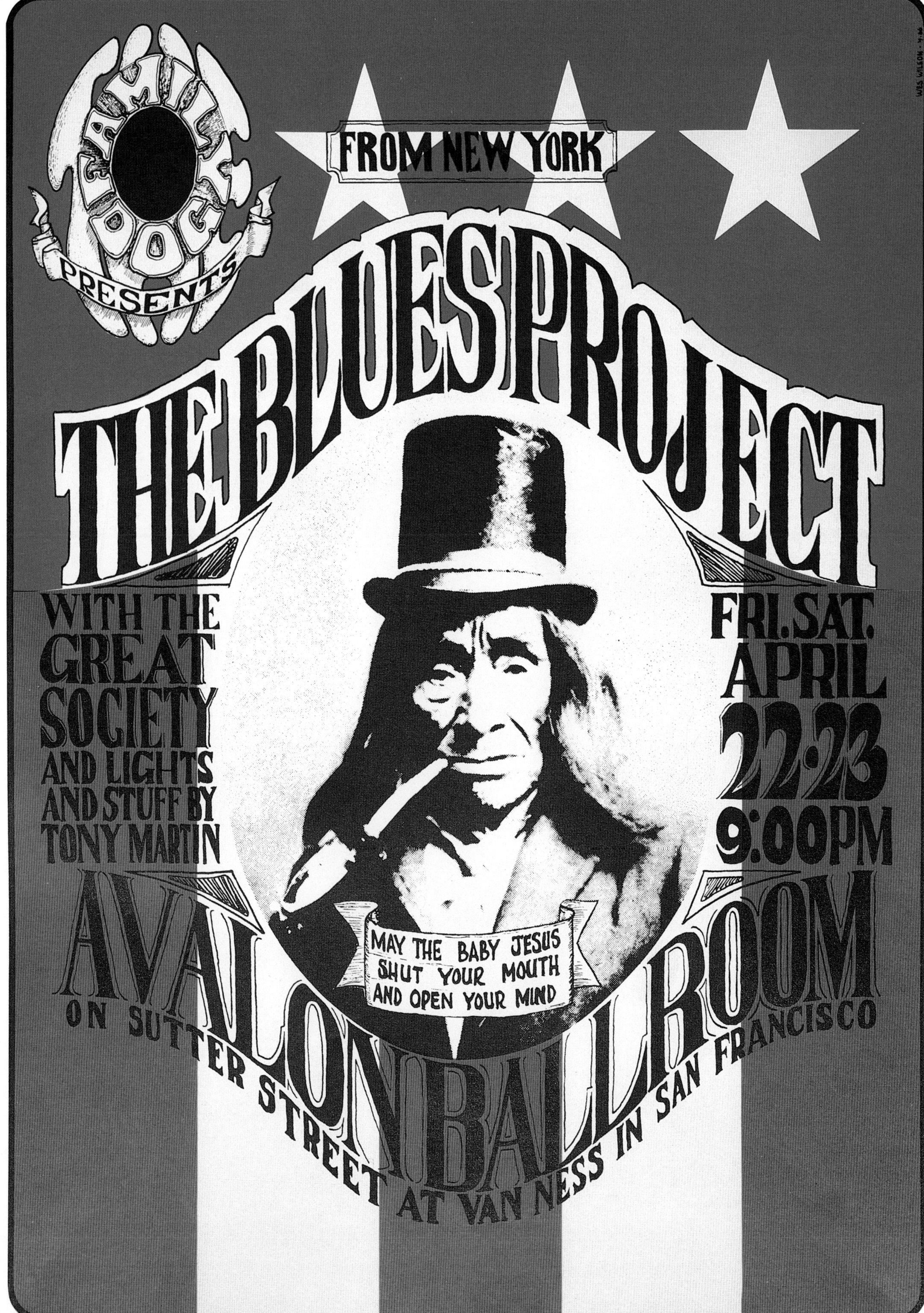
FAMILY DOG
PRESENTS
FROM NEW YORK
THE BLUES PROJECT
WITH THE GREAT SOCIETY
AND LIGHTS AND STUFF BY TONY MARTIN
FRI. SAT. APRIL 22·23 9:00PM
MAY THE BABY JESUS SHUT YOUR MOUTH AND OPEN YOUR MIND
AVALON BALLROOM
ON SUTTER STREET AT VAN NESS IN SAN FRANCISCO
WES WILSON

The Bindweed Press

FAMILY DOG
PRESENTS
THE
QUICK
SILVER
MESSENGER
SERVICE
& THE
GREAT
SOCIETY
SEPT
9-10
BALLROOM
- SANFRANCISCO
POSTER DESIGN: MOUSE! STUDIOS
TICKET OUTLETS:
SAN FRANCISCO THE PSYCHEDELIC SHOP; CITY LIGHTS BOOKS; BALLY LO; CEDAR ALLEY COFFEE HOUSE; MNASIDIKA; DISCOUNT RECORDS (North Beach); SANDAL MAKER (North Beach)
SAUSALITO TIDES BOOK SHOP; SANDAL MAKER
BERKELEY RECORD CITY, 234 Telegraph Avenue
MENLO PARK KEPLER'S BOOK STORE
No.25-3
© FAMILY DOG PRODUCTIONS, 1725 WASHINGTON STREET, SAN FRANCISCO

THE GREAT ! SOCIETY

THE GRASS ROOTS

BIG BROTHER & THE HOLDING CO.

QUICK SILVER MESSENGER SERVICE

SATURDAY FEB.★26

FILLMORE AUD.★9 pm

No. 2-2

whether joy or sorrow predominated.

The vocal portion of "White Rabbit" is only about a minute and a half long, so the obvious thing to do was to begin with a long, building, Bolero-like solo section, leading to the vocal. This we did, and that song never failed to work up a crowd.

Donahue used to come by the club and listen to a set almost every night, so it wasn't long before he heard the new material. He was still on the outside looking in at the hippie scene, although he was beginning to change; he claimed his doctor had "prescribed" marijuana for him, and he smoked it almost constantly. Also, I think he was discovering L.S.D. in those days. In any case, he wanted us to record David's good-timey "That's How It Is" for our first single. We all rebelled. I like the song now, but then, it seemed so bubblegum that Grace barely consented to sing it in the set, and we all, David included, refused to record it as a single.

Instead, we picked "Somebody to Love", which we would back with another new song of mine, a raga-rock tune named "Free Advice". "Free Advice" featured David singing lead, and Grace doing a sort of scat-Indian vocal all around the main melody. The backing instruments were bass, drums, and me twanging away on a specially tuned guitar which sounded vaguely eastern. The words, again inspired by an unhappy Leslie, were:

Woman says she loves me
She gives me free advice
I wonder who it is she loves
If she wants me to be so nice?

Tom agreed to our plan, and we headed for the studio to cut our first single. We went in to Golden State Recorders, and set up the equipment. I think they were using a state of the art four track recorder, so we were to do bass, drums, and rhythm guitar on the first pass. We decided to record "Somebody" first.

"Ready?" asked the engineer.

After maybe a minute of random diddling on our instruments, I received affirmative nods from the others, and said, "Okay."

"Okay, hit it!" said the engineer.

We played our hearts out into the tape machine, really going for it. As the last note rang out, we felt drained, but triumphant.

"Sorry, I messed up," said the engineer, "can you give it to me again?"

Feeling real anguish, we tried again, but the mood was gone. I don't know how long we stood there trying, but I know we did way more than fifty takes, and I've heard the number five hundred bandied about, before we got one that was at least okay. Nobody offered us any possibility of splicing or overdubbing as a way out of the problem, and we were too inexperienced to know anything. At some point Sly walked out of the session, disgusted by our lack of professionalism.

We took a break, and later I came back to record the solo. I tuned up, smoked a joint, turned the amp up to ten, which I had never even tried before, and without touching a string, I waited with the headphones on for the solo section to come up. When it arrived, I played the first note, actually a triple stop a la Chuck Berry, and the sound was so loud, a mighty wind coming off my speakers, that I was knocked backwards, and played the whole solo reeling around the room, still reacting to that first note! The engineer managed to record it, and we all decided it was a keeper. Later, Tom was somewhat dubious when he heard it.

During another break in the recording process, Sly brought Billy Preston into the studio. Billy was playing keyboards in Ray Charles' band, and he was starting to work with the Beatles, where he would soon be identified as the "5th Beatle"; he played the main keyboard parts on "Lady Madonna", and "Get Back", to name a few. Sly introduced us, and he and Sly began showing each other, and us, some of the cool tricks they had been picking up. Billy described some recording techniques with the Leslie, the rotating speaker for the Hammond B3 organ, and Sly demonstrated a stiff-wristed style of playing drums wherein every stroke is held in contact with the drum-skin and not allowed to bounce: very funky.

The recording of "Free Advice" went much more smoothly than "Somebody", the only bug being that, because of the open-tuned guitar, the song was pitched lower than David's best range. It was perfect for Grace, though, and the guitar, so David graciously accepted the situation. He walked over to the engineer.

"I want to try lying down on that couch and singing."

"You mean for practice, or for recording?" asked the incredulous engineer.

"For recording. It helps me relax my stomach and diaphram, and I think I can hit those low notes better that way."

"Okay. Hang on a second. I want to move the couch nearer so we can still see each other through the window." He dragged the couch over and David lay down on it. The big studio mike was lowered down to just above David's face, and, with his hands behind his head in complete relaxation, he sang it in one take.

Grace, likewise, got it on the first pass, and decided to keep her off-the-wall ending, which many would have considered a mistake.

By early spring of '66, Jerry, Grace and I had decided to replace Bard on bass. Rightly or wrongly, we thought he was not committed enough to improvement as a musician, and that we all were. David assented. I called up my friend, Peter Van Gelder who was living in Madison, Wisconsin. Peter played sax and flute, and enough keyboard to write with.

"What are you doin' these days?" I asked him.

"I'm living in a house just outside of Madison, that's where you've reached me now. I'm playing with a little jazz group here. My friend Sam is sharing the house with me ,and playing drums in the group." (Sam had been the Charlatan's first drummer.)

"We've got a rock and roll band going here," I said, "and we're doing lots of improvisation. We're playing to full houses in all the halls around here, and we've got a record contract and everything. If I sent you the money for the plane ticket, would you want to come back out here and play bass with us?"

"Sure, man. I've been playing stand-up a little bit here, and it wouldn't be any problem for me to learn the electric bass."

"Okay, cool," I said, "I can teach you where all the notes are and shit like that. We've left a whole month open with no gigs, so you've got time to learn."

We finalized the details, and he flew out. One month to learn how to play an instrument, and a band's entire repertoire? He actually did it, and did a pretty damned good job. He stayed with me while I taught him the rudiments of bass playing. The band stopped playing gigs for a month, and then we started up again with Peter.

This gave us some very dramatic options. On "White Rabbit", for example, Grace would start out playing the bass (and she played aggressive, powerful bass) while Peter soloed on soprano sax. Certainly, at that time, I had never heard a soprano used in a rock and roll band, and its high, reedy sound was perfect for rock and roll. After Peter played, I would play a guitar solo, and at the climax of the instrumental passage, Grace would hand the bass to Peter, and she would begin singing; people loved it. On Eden Abba's classic "Nature Boy", Peter played silver flute while Grace played recorder, their parts curling in and out of each other's, while I played chords and a bass part on my lowest guitar strings.

Peter's first gig with us was at the Avalon Ballroom when we shared the bill with the Blues Project. The Project blew us off the stand, though the crowd seemed to like us a lot, and, as a direct result, Peter wrote "Arbitration".

Our rehearsal house, which was also where Peter and his wife Marsha and David and I lived, was on McAlister Street, in the Fillmore district. The neighborhood was populated by relativly poor black people living in the old victorian style buldings which lined its streets. It wasn't considered a very prestigious neighborhood, but in my few months of living there, I never saw, or heard of, one crime occurring.

We had the instruments set up in the living room in a big circle. It was Monday, the 17th of March, 1966 (I cheated and figured out the date from the poster of our Avalon gig). Jerry was talking.

"I've got to hand it to you, man. You didn't play perfectly last night, none of us did. But you did an amazingly good job. "Thanks, man..... But, shit! The Blues Project was so fuckin' powerful! We've got to be more like that. We've got too many people playing the same notes in the same range with the same rhythm. If we can play more like counter-point, and in different ranges, our sound'll get a lot bigger. And we've got to make stuff build more, too; not just start everything at once. I've been working on this new song, and I'd like to try it out today.

The song was "Arbitration." In "Arbitration", the emphasis was on ensemble harmony playing, and building by adding elements. The song utilizes changing scales and time signatures, but the power comes from the layering of the parts. This song marked a turning point for us, and affected everything we played. Even the older material was revised to make the parts more pared down and clear, yet more effective by their relative positionings.

With his melodic and musically knowledgeable bass playing, his sax and flute solos, and his songwriting, Peter added an incredible amount to the Great Society and, I think, to the whole San Francisco scene. We were now in the period of the Great Society that I remember most fondly. The scene was powerful and flourishing, but on a national level, was still only the dream destination of some Los Angeles, flower-haired crooner.

THE RECORDING STUDIO SESSION
Photographs © 1966 by Ray Andersen

L. to R. Jerry (drums), Bard, Grace,
John Carpenter, David, Darby

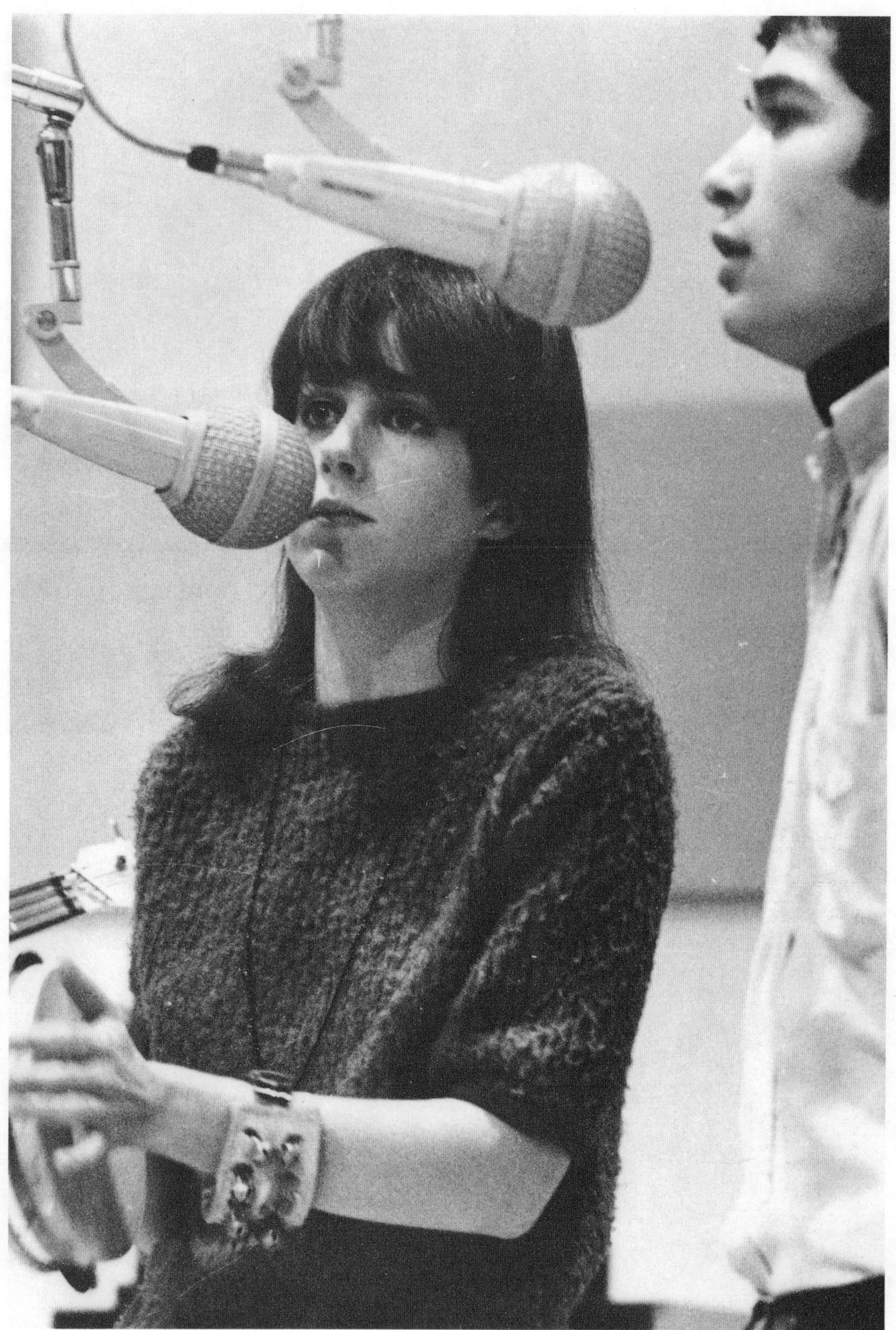

Grace, David

L. to R. Bard, Darby, John, Grace, David

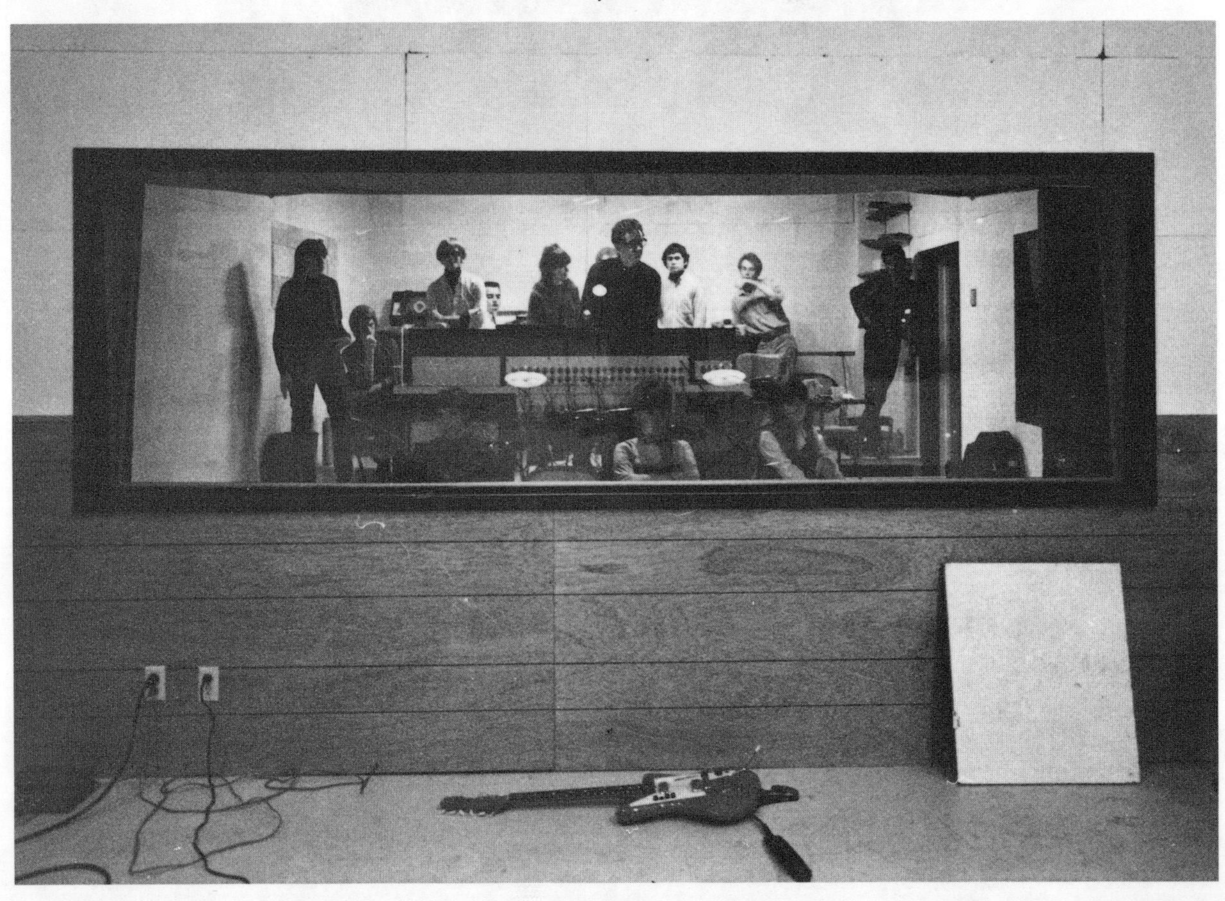

Band & friends

Jerry

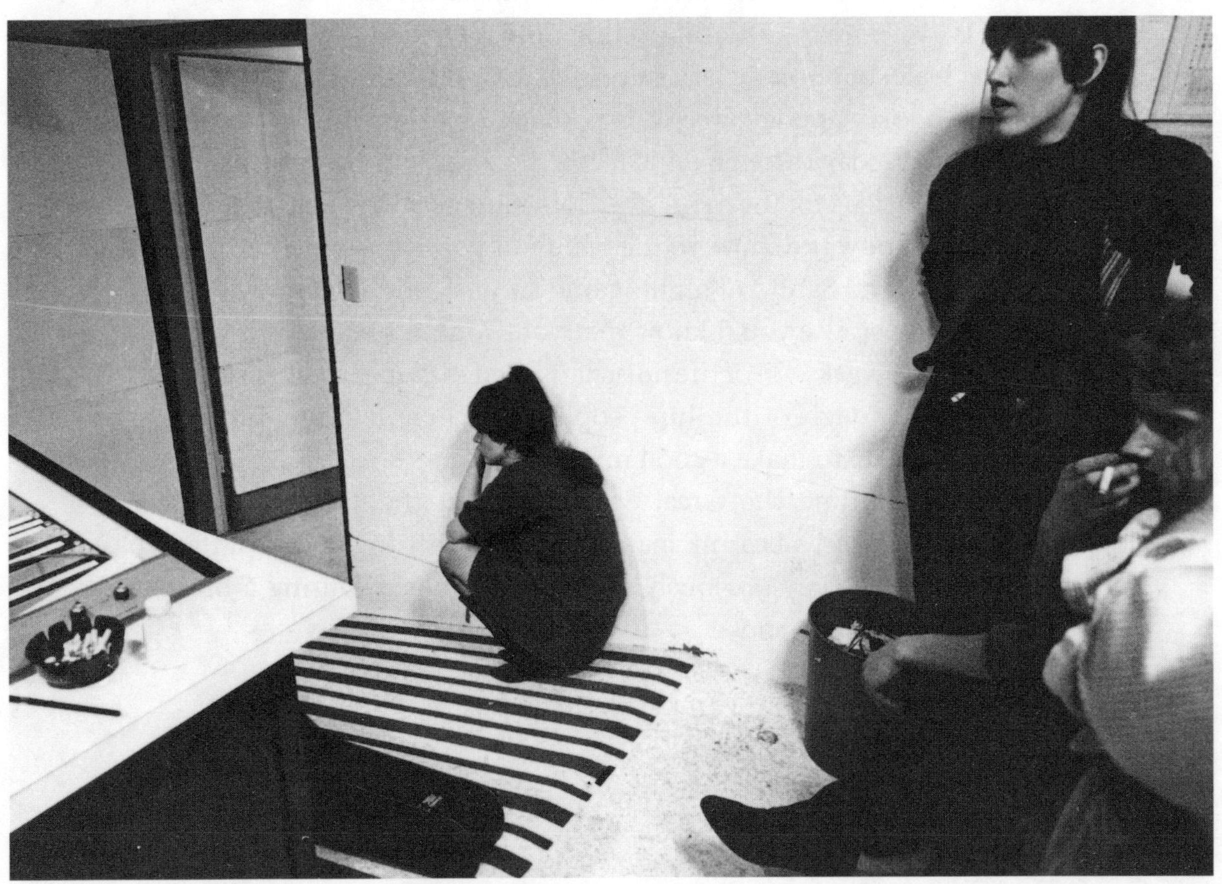

Grace, Leslie, Darby

8

Matrix

There was really only one hippie nightclub in San Francisco, the Matrix. It was started by Marty Balin as an outlet for his group the Jefferson Airplane, and the booking policy, at least in the early days, seemed to center completely on the hippie bands. Our band liked to play there. We liked the club. The money wasn't great. We were in the union at the time, and we had to pay dues as if we were getting scale, but no one was getting that kind of money there. Nonetheless, the booking policy was really cool for a local band. The preferred gig there ran Tuesday through Sunday. As the week wore on, the band would really be tuned up for the room, and the sound person would have the levels wired, and know the show, so the band was going to sound it's best by the time Friday and Saturday nights came around. Sunday night was always kind of sad because you'd know that you wouldn't be playing there for a month or six weeks. All of the musicians used to come by and listen to each other, and enough of the hip people were there, along with plenty of straight people, to make a good mix.

The first time the Great Society played the Matrix, I noticed a handsome couple, a beatnik man and woman, sitting at one of the tables near the stage. They obviously enjoyed our music. During a break, as I walked by, the man spoke.

"Hey, man you guys sound pretty good. Would you like a beer?"

They were William and Patricia Reid. We had a short conversation, and they invited us to visit them in their Potrero Hill Victorian house. I accepted. Jerry and Grace had lived on Potrero Hill, as had our friend Doug, so it was fun to go back to the old neighborhood again.

The house was tall and narrow, and they had divided it from top to bottom right down the middle, and had rented out the south half; they lived in the north three floors. A large, middle eastern palm stood in the front yard. At their invitation, I walked up a narrow flight of stairs and into their living room , to the left of the stairs. The room was immaculately clean, and almost spartanly laid out. Art objects that they had bought while making a round-the-world trip were displayed with great care. Young as I was, and naive, I had never seen an example of art integrated into living space. The artists I knew all lived in great jumbles of mess, and the "straight" people (we used this term to designate non-hipness, not necessarily sexual orientation) lived in a sterile, lack-of-art. William and Pat had worked hard to make their house, from the exterior paint to the toilet paper holders, cry, `good art.' Also, Patricia was a gourmet cook, and kept her fine body tight with Yoga. Her long, black hair, and beautiful face shone with health.

William was a painter. His reddish hair and beard were beginning to grey; his beard was a wonder upon his even features. Each hair grew out parallel to those around it, with no curling or odd angles anywhere. To complete it, he trimmed it to the perfection of good sculpture. He smiled often, and he spoke his words with the slight and pleasant drawl of the midwest.

I don't know the right words to characterize his work; it is not so abstract that it is difficult to recognize the people, animals, and objects he portrays, nor is it simply realistic. He makes wonderful use of curves and straight lines, and color. His work has influenced my music more than that of any other non-musician. I often close my eyes when I play, and try to imitate his sense of line with my music lines. His paintings hang in some of the best galleries in Europe, and in the collections of some knowledgeable Americans. I don't know a lot about the placement of his pictures, because he is shyly reluctant to talk about it; what I do know, is from a mutual friend, Richard Opaterny.

Richard taught ballet in the Palo Alto area. Carol, the woman who would become my wife, was one of his students. Richard sent his graduates to some of America's top ballet companies: Harkness, Joffrey, and San Francisco, among them. He got into the hippie scene early on, and was one of its shining lights. William offered to do posters for us, and I was delighted to accept, where I could; most often, we were not invited to be involved with the poster process. The Matrix, however, allowed us to choose, and William soon produced a poster which I loved for our next appearance there. It depicted an opening red and white drug capsule with stars pouring out. He did other cool posters as time went on.

William had grown up in St. Louis, had often heard Lester Young play live, and had met him. He turned me on to Lester's playing, and this, too, influenced me. I loved the way he played behind the beat, but never dragging, and with sweet tone and vibrato.

Usually there would be two bands on the bill at the Matrix, and I remember one of the times we were there with the Dead, and I walked back into the musicians area, which wasn't a musicians room really, it was just a large kitchen-store room at the back of the club, and as I walked through the door back there, this young woman said, "Well, look at Mr. big time.", and I looked over, and it was my high school sweetheart, my first real love, Sarah, who by this time had married Jerry Garcia, although I hadn't known it. And it was just another example of how all of these worlds seemed connected in one way or another. The connection just reached from one person to the next in the early days of the San Francisco rock scene.

The stage at the Matrix was tiny, and none of the instruments was miked; actually, the whole club was tiny. A bar ran along the left side of the club, and the rest was taken up by small round tables, with the stage in the right, rear corner. The place changed look several times, but the most psychedelic was done in moire patterns. Otherwise, it was just a small, nondescript bar. Dancing was not allowed at the Matrix. California had a morality police force named the A.B.C. (Alcoholic Beverage Control). They required clubs to get a license from them permitting dancing, but, for no reason other than their own sense of morality, they seldom gave out the licenses. The dark ages are so close behind us.

The sound and light show booth was a little, box-like room to the left and up in the air four or five feet from the entrance. It was up because it had been "built" directly over toilet fixtures without removing them! Here, tape recorders captured the performances of virtually every band that played the club. Many of these tapes still exist, unreleased.

It's hard to believe now, how sophisticated we felt, how seriously we took ourselves. On the other hand, I know I for one, was playing at life; playing at being an adult, a hippie, a musician. I don't think I was unique in this. Sometimes I would discuss this feeling with close friends, and no one ever said, "You're weird; I feel completely adult." Early on in my relationship with Leslie, one of our favorite songs was Chuck Berry singing, "It was a teenage wedding, and the old folks wished them well." We were not teenagers, we were not married, and the old folks did not wish us well, but, man, we loved that song!

One day, my brother got a call from our friend, Chet Helms. He was, along with his other projects, managing a group that he had been "hiding away" in the middle of the Haight. He was always talking about them, but very few people had heard them play; they hadn't worked anywhere. Chet had gotten hold of the Matrix to show his new group. I think it was by invitation only, and as I remember, most of the band people came. Chet had been hyping the group to us all, individually, for some time. He was especially high on the group's lead guitarist, James Gurley. Chet said that James lived with the guitar in his hands. Years latter, John Cipollina's sister, Sheesh, said to me, "What is it with you guitar players, you practice so much!" And you know, she's right, guitar players tend to be fanatical about practicing. Anyway, the night came to go to the Matrix, and hear this new group Big Brother and the Holding Company.

Outside the club, I stood scraping some gum off of the sole of my Flagg Brothers Beatle boots. The sole had a hole in it, so I could only scrape in one direction, away from the hole. I was standing there, in the street, sort of pawing at the curb, like a bull about to charge, when Garcia walked up. He walked almost like a sailor, slightly bow-legged, and with a rolling motion.

His face was lit up with a smile, and he seemed very at peace with himself. He wore a dark blue Navy pea coat, black jeans and Beatle boots. His face, like mine, was somewhat pock-marked.

"I bet on the curb," he said.

"Fucking bubble-gum," was my clever rejoinder. "Heard this guy play?" I asked.

"Yeh," he said, "He's cool." His voice rose and fell on the words "He's" and "cool", showing, I thought, total acceptance and respect, but not necessarily an abundance of personal enthusiasm. There was in his manner, his attitude and speech, something that reminded me of W. C. Fields: a humorous irony that was not malicious. For some reason, perhaps because I had continued scraping the curb making "feet" the focus, he did about one bar of soft-shoe before walking, smiling and nodding, into the club.

The air was thick with fog, and chilly. From here on lower Fillmore St., you could hear the loud, bass voices of the old fog horns. A large, black and brown, scruffy dog trotted up to my green, '54 Chevy, a car which I loved, but did not treat as a classic, more as a sort of a tank for the streets, and smelled the rear, passenger-side tire before moving on. The sidewalk, street, and a vacant lot nearby, were all littered with paper and rusting cans and broken glass. Jukebox rock and roll from the club across the corner on the same side of the street, the Pierce St. Annex, swirled with the fog, and dim yellow street-light, and harsh white security-light, into a kind of city soup. I loved the very dirt of the place, it was so far from the middle class Palo Alto from which I had escaped. The evil of the city-bred robber, stealing for food or rent, or even for drugs, seemed noble compared with that of the Peninsula good-old-boys, who so politely tolerated, and even respected, blacks who stayed in their place. Here, in the City, I was Sam Spade, Holden Caulfield, and Keith Richards; I was a Black, Junkie, Musical Explorer. I was Robin Hood. Naturally, I had smoked a joint in the car before arriving. Now, wanting alcohol, I rocked my head back and forth a few times to crack my neck, and walked under the large, hand-painted playbill sign into the club. The contrast was almost alarming: from the cool, wet, jazz-mood of the street, into the hot, nervous-cigarette, babbling-hippie, promote-promote club, and it was a club.

My friend, Ray Andersen, was booking the acts, doing the sound and lights, hiring bouncers and bartenders: running the place. Ray was a lover of art movies. I had met him at San Francisco State in the film department. I don't know if he had actually been enrolled there, I know I hadn't, but that too was a "club" and all it took was a love of film to belong. We used to show each other movie clips, some public domain, some pirated, and talk about editing, framing, sound, and all of the aspects of movie making that we were aware of. If a new art movie opened, we were likely to meet, unplanned, at the theater. We saw "Sundays and Cibelle", "David and Lisa", "The Seven Samurai", on and on. When some of Jordan Bellson's works were presented at Foothill College in Palo Alto, we drove down to see them and meet the film maker. Bellson's abstract film works were mind boggling; among other techniques, he featured a careful use of after-images. In a crude example of my own invention, if he showed you a strong yellow circle, the next frames might consist of deep purple background, otherwise blank, but you would continue to "see" the yellow circle. In this way, a lot of what you "saw" in his movies wasn't actually there. Bellson's films had titles like "Miosis", and, somehow, seemed to shift your perception between a cellular and a cosmic view.

Ray stood about 5 feet 10, had thin, sandy hair, talked and used his body very animatedly and was interested in just about everything. In a typical gesture, he would rotate his head downwards until his chin contacted his chest, raise his brows, and look at you as if over the tops of glasses which he only now has begun to wear. The flow of his conversation was almost stream of consciousness, and could be difficult, or even occasionally, impossible, to follow, especially on the telephone. He might make reference to almost anything from the stroke styles of French Impressionist painting to the power fluctuations found in house current, quite tangentially. Some of his sentences and paragraphs were as thick with obtuse reference as those of James Joyce. If he wanted to disagree with you, which he only sometimes did (he was coming more from a happy abundance of experience than from negativity) he would say something like, "Well, I don't know," and then be off into an idea stew of vast complexity which hinted, often subtly, at another point of view. This lack of direct, "straight", communication was one of the features of the hippie era, and was practiced somewhat differently by each of us. Perhaps, this was an outgrowth of language patterns that we had started in early in our lives; I know that in high school, my friends and I used sarcasm in almost every sentence. The only hippie rule seemed to be, as with clothes, hair cuts, cars, houses, you name it, "Anything But Straight."

As I walked towards Jerry and Grace's table, located in the most desired part of the club, between the bar and the stage, but not too close, Ray scurried by me, shuffling along sideways, with his shoulders hunched up and his hands rubbing each other. He muttered something to me, at me?, which I did not understand. Fortunately, he did not seem to expect a reply, but continued on to the stage, where he placed a microphone in the stand waiting there. He looked out at the room, nervously, over the tops of his imaginary glasses, as he quickly uncoiled a cord for the microphone he had just placed. The club was full and noisy, with a definite air of expectation; you could hear the buzz you've heard of.

Chet Helms then came out of the musician's room, and took the stage. He was tall and thin, with long thin straight blond hair and a long blond curly beard. He wore a tan suit of western cut, and a paisley shirt with long collar. He tried to adjust the microphone stand upwards to accommodate himself, but failed. He was forced to hunch over the mike in what must have been an uncomfortable position. How many times would I see him repeat these behaviors? He boomed out a smiling, "Hello! Welcome to the show!" He told us how great the band was, how great each member of the band was, how great the club was, how great we all were, how great life was, and, by the way, did I tell you how great this band is?, for about 15 minutes. Almost all of us were friends of his, so naturally we began to heckle him.

Finally, he left the stage and the band came out. They played with aggression and with an extremely treble sound. James Gurley played with finger picks and therefore played twice as fast as anybody else on the local scene, even on their fast songs. Their music most strongly foreshadowed the punk movement. They had a very down home, just folks quality, which I came to know was real. Peter Albin, the bass player, sang lead on most of the songs. I really liked their music and their attitude; whatever this San Francisco thing was, they deserved to be part of it. We were very chauvinistic about our scene. Anything that smacked of penetration from the outside or of commercial exploitation was abhorrent.

Big Brother's only weakness seemed to be in the vocals. I think a lot of people told Chet that if the group was going to become really popular, the singing would have to be better; I know I heard people express this opinion to each other. Nonetheless, I don't want to paint this opening as a downer in any way; people were very excited, and it was obvious that the local scene had another powerful group to bolster it.

The Jefferson Airplane, the Matrix's premiere band, had decided on some changes of style. Their harmonies and chord changes had come right out of commercial folk music. They were good. I don't know how or why they decided to emphasize the rock side of their style, but they did. Their drummer, Skip, just sort of wandered away from the scene. I remember standing at the back of the Fillmore with him and he told me that he wanted to get away. It wasn't the band or the music, it was just the need to move. I couldn't believe that anyone would walk away from all this. The local adulation alone was blowing my mind. The torrent of love, joy, and almost worship that washed up onto the stage was heady stuff to me. Then too, we all seemed poised on the verge of national recognition, and with it, hit records. Our music on the same stations with Dion and the Belmonts! I could be wrong, but I think it was drugs that made Skip split: people with drug and alcohol problems often feel the need to change the external circumstances of their lives.

One morning I was sitting at the kitchen table of my then womanfriend in the Haight, and out of one of the bedrooms walked a guy with the other woman who shared the apartment. He was dressed, but his hair was still messed up, and he was rubbing sleep out of his eyes.

He yawned words while stretching his shoulders back, and rolling his head to the side, "How' you doin'?"

Catching his yawn, I replied, also yawning and stretching, "Okay, man." He sat down at the table with me, and the two women walked off, quietly talking and laughing together.

Over coffee and a joint he told me that he was the Airplane's new drummer. His name was Spencer Dryden. He was fresh out of L.A. and Vegas, but he wore it well. He had the charm of a traveling salesman, and

I had no doubt that he could really play. He could! He was not big and strong as are many rock and roll drummers, and I think he had to force himself to play hard (loud) in those early, unmiked days. The coolest thing about him, and his playing, was that you could see his commitment to the rhythm of the song at all times. It was almost as if he sat dancing on his stool, and the drumming was the logical extension of that dance.

Did they fire the bass player, or did he quit? I don't know. I first met the new guy, Jack Casady, in the dumpy old second floor balcony musician's room at the Fillmore. We were on the bill together that night, and apropos of his name, he was really jacked. It was his first gig with the group, and he knew that this scene was happening. Nobody introduced us, but I said hello to him, and he introduced himself to me, and the ice was broken and soon he and Grace and all of us were talking the quick, almost meaningless hip phrases at each other.

He had some little practice amp, and was warming up, tuning up, getting himself and his bass ready. I loved his playing right from the start, and so did everybody else who came within earshot. I remember the first riff I heard him play: five, one pause, one, two, three pause. He would slide from the five note down to the one, then play one, two, and slide from the two note up to the three note. He would finish the phrase by making the three note sing with subtle violinish vibrato.

In his overall style, He played more notes than was traditional in rock and roll, as did all of the San Francisco bass players, but he chose very sweet notes, and left big airy holes for them to breath. Phil Lesh was more inclined towards dissonances, and our own Peter Van Gelder tended to pick notes similar in scale to Jack's, but both of them were far busier than he was. I think all three were great bass players, and I don't take anything away from Peter Albin, whose playing I also loved. All of these people could make their styles work, and that's the real test. They sounded enough alike so that someone could have easily done a recognizable parody of the San Francisco sound, but actually, the genre was big enough for them all to have plenty of individual expression.

One day, I started seeing people at the Matrix wearing buttons with the words, "The Jefferson Airplane Loves You" printed on them; they were giving them out as a promotional device. To us this seemed hokey and saccharine, so, I don't remember which of us thought of it, we had buttons made stating, " The Great Society Doesn't Like You Very Much At All". Of course, this was a joke on the Airplane's button, but it also hinted that Lyndon's ideas might not be as benign for all citizens as touted.

One of my favorite local groups was the Sons of Champlin, whom I first saw perform at the Matrix. They could really play and sing. Perhaps their weakest aspect was their song writing, but they had a great blend of R & B with jazz, gospel and rock and roll. They played with exuberance and with much more competence than any other San Francisco band. Bill (Champlin) knew many Ray Charles songs and he could get the cool, bending inflections into his voice that are required to make that style cook. Terry Hagerty, the lead guitar player, played fast and cleanly, and with a knowledge of scales beyond that of any other local. He brought a jazz sensibility to the music, but with that R.&B. feel, something like that of Cannonball Aderley and others of that ilk. The band could sure make a crowd feel good; they had all of the appeal of a great bar band, but with loads of originality and depth.

When Bill (Champlin) invited Peter and me to their house way out in West Marin, he and I quickly accepted; for one thing, we had no dope. I drove us from our Mill Valley hill-top house out to the freeway, then north to the Sir Francis Drake exit, and on out into the country with its rolling green hills, cows, horse ranches, and golf courses. We talked tensely, and I smoked Pall Malls almost constantly because, we had no dope. We weren't broke. Something had happened, something that was supposed to happen, hadn't, I don't know.

We arrived at the house about noon on a spring day. It was early in the year, so the weather was perfect; summer could get pretty hot around there. A large dog slept under a weeping willow tree, and barely raised his head to look at us as we walked towards the house.

An open, screen door led into a kitchen, and on into a darkened living room, set up for music. No one answered our, "Hello?" as we walked in. On a small drink-ringed table, was an open cigar box with dope and papers. We sat down and rolled a joint. Several minuets later, Terry Hagerty walked in, followed by Bill Champlin a short time later. We thanked them for the smoke, which Terry acknowledged by smiling and raising a hand, palm toward us. Soon another friend came in, a wonderful drummer named John (nicknamed Fuzzy for his huge growth of curly black hair), and we started to play some basic blues.

"Alright. That was really cool," said Fuzzy, when the first "song" had come to an end. "Hey, what color is my shirt?" this was his (to me, humorous) way of saying look at my shirt.

We jammed for a few hours, playing sometimes inspired music, and stopped once to sit outside in the beautiful green, brown and blue nature, for a while. Then, Peter and I drove back to our own music house, with a pocket full of joints.

I saw other local groups perform at the Matrix; the Sopwith Camel (why so happy all the time?), Country Joe and the Fish (reminded me of The Mystery Trend musically, in that they changed major and minor chords in ways that "broke the rules"), and others.

During the course of this year, 1966, San Francisco became more famous for its new sound, and musicians from other cities started to play the Matrix. The Butterfield Band came and he and Mike Bloomfield blew us all away. The sheer competence of the band was awesome on this scene. I had never heard guitar tone as good as Bloomfield got out of that Goldtop Les Paul. I thought it must have a hollowed-out cavity in it to make it resonate and sustain so with that mid-rangey almost horn sound. I just loved it! During the show, a friend, I think it was Chet Helms, told me that he was having a little party for the Butterfield band, and he invited us (the Great Society) to come. Peter and I agreed, and after the show, we went to the address Chet had given us.

The house was in San Francisco, but the wet, brick walkway was bordered by a jungle of plants, and rain dripped and ran off of the many large leaves around us. An alive, earth smell radiated up at us, bringing the tropics to mind, even in the swirling San Francisco fog. The smell of the joint we were smoking blended perfectly with the wet smells of the garden. Inside the house were a few friends, four or five young women of obvious beauty, and Michael Bloomfield and Elvin Bishop. Bloomfield and Bishop were sitting on a couch. They had their guitars out, electric guitars, and were playing without amplification. They were not playing to amuse people, in fact, you had to listen very closely to hear what they were playing, and no one but Peter and I seemed that interested; I think the others were happy just to be in the same room with these celebrities. Bloomfield was giving Bishop a kind of advanced guitar lesson. He was showing him how to imitate a horn section on the guitar.

"Dig it," he was saying, "This is what it looks like in `A'." The voicings he was using were similar to those Steve Croper would use on the beginning of "Soul Man". These guys had just played their hearts out for hours, and had paused only long enough for a crosstown drive before getting into it again. Bishop was fascinated, showing total concentration and desire to learn, coupled with a real respect for Bloomfield. The whole scene was just beautiful to me. The groupies, the master, the student(s): the bullshit and the real.

I first saw Steve Miller play at the Matrix, and, again, craftsmanship was abundant. I had never heard a bass player groove as simply yet effectively as did the dude he brought, Lonnie.

It feels as if I have spent a thousand nights in the Matrix listening to the most beautiful music on the planet, and about ten minutes there listening to stuff I didn't like, but I may have these time values reversed or out of proportion, and I'm not really sure that I was the one who was there listening, or if I just heard about it or dreamt it or something.

9

The Middle Days

My first experience with a light show was an extremely powerful one. A friend of mine named Oscar was a self-taught musician; intellectually, he didn't know from nothing about music. He also didn't know really any chords on the guitar, but he had a tremendous gift for melody, and a burning spirit, which came out in his playing. I used to take drugs with him, and occasionally, I would hear him play a little guitar.

One day, he told me that he had begun playing with a light show in a small private studio set up for that purpose in the Fillmore district. He invited me to come, and I was happy to accept. I met him at the address he had given me, and we walked in together. The room was about as large as a middle-sized living room. The walls were painted black, and the lighting was indirect and subdued. Large, flat pillows were scattered about on the black floor. On the north wall was a movie screen about seven feet high and twelve feet long. We, the seven or eight people assembled, shared a couple of fat joints.

Oscar began to change the strings on his acoustic steel-string guitar as we all smoked. "I change them every time I play," he said, "I can't stand the sound of dead strings, and they die so fast!.....Oh, I don't change them if I'm going to stay home, but here (he laughed and held out his free right hand palm up), I want it to sound good, man."

Directly opposite the screen, was a projector and a small table full of glass dishes and vials of dyes.

At some cue that I missed, the lights dimmed to blackness, Oscar began playing his guitar, and the light show began. If you have not seen a light show in this sort of intimate environment, you have not seen one as it should be seen. My friend Ray Andersen has complained to me many times about how difficult it is to project color across a large room and have it retain any of it's vibrancy. He should know, because he worked as the light show artist at the Fillmore for a long time, billing his show as the Holy See. Here, in Bill Ham's small studio, the colors were so bright and beautiful, they could bring tears to your eyes. Oscar's playing was also very beautiful. The brilliant new strings brought out ringing overtones for each note he played. The lower strings sounded brassy, the higher strings, zingy, and the middle ones, almost like a human voice. He started slowly, and, over a period of perhaps twenty minutes, built to a feverish conclusion. Whether by prearrangement or inspiration, the light show did the same; at first, little globules of incredibly intense color sidled up to larger, more complex systems (amebas? universes?), and stroked and rubbed against them, coaxing, urging, admission. Gradually, the tempo picked up, and the colors writhed and jumped, banged and humped, merged, and radiated outward again. An almost post-orgasmic peace concluded the show. In a strictly literal sense, all other light shows that I saw were pale imitations of this first one. Sometimes, a sound is so good, and complex, you can almost taste it. Here, were colors so pure and strong and bright, that just to look upon one was a glorious experience, regardless of whether it moved, or how it was shaped; liquid stained glass, with sunlight shining directly through it.

Ray Andersen did the dancing globules too, but, at the Matrix and the Fillmore, his shows also featured film clips and still photos chosen and screened with an uncanny knowledge of the work of the musicians who were performing. Of course, when you were the musician, you didn't get to appreciate the show much; the lights were mostly just something you didn't want to blind you!

Elements kept coming together to make the San Francisco scene happen. Ironically, one of the most necessary, became the destroyer: publicity. Ralph Gleason, a San Francisco jazz critic, early on noticed that a new scene was emerging, and was intrigued by it. The connection was likely enough; the beat scene had incorporated jazz music into itself, and the hippie scene was born pretty directly out of the beat. Though neither movement could have existed without Existentialism, the hippies seemed, by and large, a happier group. Ralph wrote about the costumes, and the expanding improvisations in the music. He brought respectability to the scene, as well as sheer publicity. People who would never have thought to go to a rock and roll show began to. He told people, "This is good, this is art." I don't know if his columns were syndicated nationally, but in any case, he focused national attention on the scene very quickly.

The publicity enabled the city to support two (and sometimes more) halls, at least every Friday and Saturday night. It enabled the halls to begin hiring national acts to mix with the local ones. This mixture was artistically beneficial. For example, when the Great Society played the Avalon Ballroom with the Blues Project, we learned a tremendous amount about how to make a small group sound big through arranging and dynamics, and I think the Blues Project was encouraged by the eclectic quality of our material to further explore their own strangeness.

Chet Helms ran the Avalon. In my dealings with him, he was always kind and fair. The place was not better or worse than the Fillmore, just different. Some must have preferred one over the other, but most seemed to just go where the band they wanted to hear was. Stylistic elements mixed seemingly without fear of contextual clash; a mirrored ball threw flecks of white onto people rendered absurd by drenching pools of black light. Eras caromed. Acid and alcohol. 1930's curtains, 1830's clothes. People passed lighted joints to one another with casual caution, but it was okay; the police were staying away. Once, I was standing in the Avalon talking to the woman I was with, when I noticed that she was giving me odd sideways looks. We were standing under a black light, and when I checked myself out, I discovered that my shoulders were covered with dandruff which stood out sharply in the black light. I wanted to be cool, and I knew that cool people didn't worry about such things as dandruff, so I laughed and said "far out", but I soon moved us away from where we had been standing.

The first night Janis played with Big Brother, was at the California Hall, one of the local halls used by the hip promoters in the early days. I can't remember if we were on the bill with them that night, but I sure remember the show. Her strong, gritty voice was immediately obvious, but even more apparent, was her ability to win over a crowd. It was nearly impossible not to stare constantly at her. She pranced, she strutted, she shrieked, she whispered. The word of mouth was, a star is born.

I met Janis repeatedly in people's Haight area houses, but it is at the Avalon that I remember her best. The famous Jim Marshall photo of her half-reclining on the couch with the bottle of Southern Comfort, doesn't really look posed to me; I often saw her in just that position. She was usually very up, right before performing, laughing, especially at herself, in a way that was irresistible. We were on the bill a bunch of times with her and Big Brother at the Avalon, and at the Fillmore. She and Grace got along very well in the musician's rooms, Grace with her cheap champagne, Janis with her Southern Comfort. It's interesting that with all of the "recreational" drugs then popular, alcohol was most performers' favorite for its nerve calming properties.

Big Brother was about to go on, and Grace and Janis were talking.

"You're so pretty," Janis said, smiling broadly and shaking her head from side to side. "How do you make your hair look like that?"

"Fuck, I don't know," Grace laughed and spoke simultaneously. "I just moeshe it around with my fingers, and spray shit at it."

"And look at my fuckin' knee," Janis said, pointing at a two inch sore, "I burned it on a Goddamned motorcycle exhaust pipe."

"No one ever sees my knees," Grace laughed, "except Jerry and maybe the guys in the band." She always wore either a black leotard, or a pants-suit.

Grace drank from her small bottle of champagne in its brown paper bag; she could just as easily remove it from the bag here, but she didn't; either she liked it that way, or it just didn't occur to her. Actually, she always left it in the bag, except when she was at home. Janis took the top off her Southern Comfort, drank some from the bottle, then replaced the top. Each time she drank, she removed and then replaced the top, as if she was either afraid that some of the precious fluid might spill, or she thought that she was finished drinking.

"Want to try some of this?" she said, holding the bottle towards Grace.

"No thanks." Grace said, cringing, then smiling, "I'll stick with my wine." She fired up a cigarette, and jumped up off the torn, red vinyl couch, to begin pacing around the room. I was holding my guitar up to my ear, and tuning it to the band who was playing, hoping that they were in tune with Grace's Farfissa organ. Sam, Big Brother's second guitar player, was sitting in a padded chair, holding his guitar and balancing a notebook full of chord symbols on his lap. In the afternoon, he had walked into the sound check, fresh from his guitar lesson. He was very excited about the orchestral, jazz chords he was learning, even though they had little or no application in Big Brother. He was working through the changes of his latest lesson, though he couldn't have been able to hear himself at all; his fingers would learn what to do and he could listen to what it sounded like later. Earlier, Grace had said, "it's great to see him so knocked out by what he's learning, almost like a puppy." He was working with total concentration, oblivious to his surroundings. "Why don't you stop fucking around and get serious," Grace teased, bumping into his legs and almost knocking his notebook down. He grinned shyly up at her, and reddened momentarily, but went quickly back to his work.

"My ass is stuck to the couch," said Janis, standing up with kind of a tearing sound, as she separated herself from the couch. "Oh well," she said, "at least fleas don't live in vinyl."

Grace sat down again; one pacer at a time. James Gurley hadn't arrived yet, and Janis suddenly said, "Where's James?" with almost panic in her voice. Peter Albin said, "He'll be here, he's cool." Sam looked up from his work, and raised his eyebrows in, I thought, a questioning way. He smiled a closed mouth non-humorous smile, and went back to work. "I hate it when people get to the gig at the last minute," said Janis, "it freaks me out."

"Yeh," said Grace, "I hate that shit too." Our own bass player, Peter and his wife Marsha were taking their small daughter to Spencer Dryden's girl friend's house in the Haight for baby sitting. This little side trip added an unwelcome element of suspense to the evening; would he arrive on time?

Jerry, Grace and I preferred to leave the band house at the same time and either ride together or caravan to the gig.

Janis remained agitated; it would be easy to describe her as a very emotional person, but we all were; everything was either wonderful, or complete shit. "Where the fuck is he?" she asked, with an intense combination of anger and fear. Peter Albin put an arm around her and said,"shhh, it's gonna be okay." She accepted his hug for a moment, but quickly broke away, I think because of nerves, not any dislike for him. I never saw the slightest hint that Janis was unhappy with the band; my impression is that her later dissatisfaction was manufactured by the record people for their own commercial goals; they would have been happier with a Las Vegas back-up band. She started sort of raking her fingers through her hair, but too violently. She was half tearing it out by the roots. Suddenly, James burst into the room. He had on tight black jeans, a black tee shirt, a shiny black leather jacket and the regulation black Beatle boots. He was about six feet tall, and looked like he weighed about 120 pounds; very skinny. His long, brown hair was kind of stringy, possibly not overly clean, and though he grinned, he looked sort of harassed, frantic and burdened. Nonetheless, the mood in the room immediately changed to supercharged joy; he was here, that was the main thing, and we were all too egocentric to stay with any possible problem of his for long. Janis greeted him like a long lost brother. "I wanna eat that audience," said Janis, "let me at 'em." Grace laughed and said," Yeh, totally, dude." or possibly something more 60'sish.

I had been hearing about this new group, the Quicksilver Messenger service, and now we were booked to be on the bill with them at the Avalon. I had known that John Cipollina was from Mill Valley, because I had met his father when I was looking for a house to rent in Mill Valley; his father was a realtor there. His father talked about how dedicated to the guitar John was, and I sensed a lot of pride in him. Before the gig, in the afternoon, I met John and David Freiberg, their bass player. I liked them both; they seemed easy going and relaxed. John immediately showed a wide open wry sense of humor, and I never personally saw him without it, although, I have heard stories of extremely infrequent and well justified bursts of anger. I have been with John in situations that would have made almost anyone angry or frustrated, and have marveled to see him smile and continue on an even keel, perhaps bemused a bit by people's absurdities and inhospitalities. Many of us seem, in life, to be on our way to the grand function; John always seemed to sense that he was already there. Twenty or so years later, John's sister Antonia (Sheesh) was playing dates as the keyboardist in my band, and John kindly let us use his Marin studio for rehearsals. Two of the large walls were completely covered with wonderful guitars that he had collected.

"Whoah," I said, "Can I try out that Mustang?"

"Hey, man, you can play whichever one you want, wherever you want. Knock yourself out," he laughed.

I played vintage Strat.s, Les Pauls, a thirty six fretted, five octave Danelctro, and other fine and rare guitars. He also encouraged me to play his then main guitar, a Carvin, and helped me to pick out one very much like it from their catalogue (cynics note; he made no money on this deal). When it arrived, he could hardly wait to try it out, and he quickly pronounced it, " A very cool guitar." He also had a collection of vintage amps that he gave me complete access to. If someone had said, "Excuse me John, can I borrow your left nut?" I don't think he would have hesitated. During this time, I had not shared a stage with him for many years, and he and I were discussing guitar playing. He talked about his philosophy, though never without joking; essentially it amounted to `Go For It', not in the sense of weird, but in the sense of no premeditation, and loud. I started to talk about mine, and he smiled at me and his eyes shone brightly and he said, "Man, I know exactly how you play."

I dropped in on a recording session he was doing for another artist. The tracks were okay, but nothing to write home about . It was three thirty in the morning, we had all worked gigs that night, the engineer was burned, and drugs had taken their toll on most, by then (I had become drug and alcohol free by this point in my life). John sat at a steel guitar, sort of diddling around on it. It seemed like the most productive thing would be to call the session, when John said, "Okay, roll the tape." The engineer did, and John proceeded to play a majestic, soaring part, that took a so-so piece, and made the whole thing really work. Then he was ready to go home. I have met a few people whose spirit seemed to completely shine, and John is one of them. But back to the Messenger Service.

My brother Jerry and Greg Elmore, their drummer, worked out the stage stuff that drummers often need to work out; where to put the kit when the other group is playing, did they want to share a kit in the interest of a speedy transition between bands, etc. They got along fine, and Jerry later told me that he really liked Greg and admired his playing.

That night, I got to hear Quicksilver. The most impressive elements to me were their harmony singing, and John's immediately distinctive vibrato style. Using a Bigsby tailpiece on his guitar, he produced a quick, shimmering vibrato, which had a very vocal quality to it. Certainly, this sound became his trademark, and it was there from the first. The band had a good, solid rhythm feel, and the singing, often in three part harmony, was strong. Again, as with Big Brother, there was never any doubt about whether this group would make it, it was, yeh, they're in.

In these middle days of '66, local bands mixed with national and international bands at shows, and at parties. There was lots of jamming of local band members together, but not a lot of jamming with people from out of town. When the Byrds came to town, for example, it was fun to party with them and discover that they weren't stuck up as some of us thought all L.A. musicians were, but no one seemed to consider playing music with them. With their electric folk style, and Dylan songbook, it would have been easy to, but the thought just didn't occur. Jeff Beck came, and it was great to meet him, but that's all that happened. Bob Dylan and The Band passed through similarly. Locals jammed, on the other hand, very frequently; I jammed regularly with members of the Sons, the Charlatans, Big Brother, and Jerry Garcia at the Page Street basement studio, Muir Beach, the Mission District loft, and various band houses and gigs. I know that we all liked playing in our own bands best, but it was fun jamming with other musicians, usually in a party atmosphere, and often with hundreds and occasionally thousands, of fellow revelers.

Avalon Knights, Fillmournings...

10

The Big Marin Bash

Do not ask where is it, let us go and make our visit. Do not ask, because I don't know; somewhere in Marin. It is the early summer of '66. We have been invited to a party to be thrown by the Dead. All of the main bands have been invited, and many of the "key" people. Here's what's weird, what happened only this once; there's to be no music. A holiday for all! This situation was very nervous-making for me; not because I was in awe of the other musicians, they were supposed to be as in awe of me as I was of them, Goddamit! What would happen, what would my role be. I was the proud possessor of what I have learned to describe as a giant ego with an inferiority complex. Really, it amounted to a hodge-podge of feelings, about half of which were unacceptable to me, and the other half, the half which I "liked", were vain to the point of silliness. I was going to have to anesthetize myself before even setting out for this party, though I would not think of it that way. I would think, "Wow, what a great party this is going to be, and as part of the party mood, I'm going to get really stoned!" I would lie to myself so quickly, so near the beginning of the thought process, that it was almost seamless. Years later, at the end of my drinking and using, these seams would all unravel, leaving me very threadbare indeed.

By this time, The Great Society was living in a large hill-top house in Mill Valley. The house had big sliding glass doors leading to a huge deck, and wooden floors throughout. Jerry and Grace had the master bedroom, Peter and his wife Marsha shared a bedroom with their two infant children, and I had a bedroom.

My room was unfurnished. I slept on a mattress with a sheet and a blanket, no bedspread. I had an ashtray, and a piece of glass onto which I put the items from my pockets when I wanted to change pants. I had no pictures or decorations, but out of the window, you could see a wonderful hillside full of trees, redwood and pine, and sometimes the fog would roll over that opposite hilltop from the other side of the hill like a wave, psychedelic like a wave, with infinite little movements, fades and manifestations, so obviously representing all of life throughout eternity: uncountable births and deaths.

I woke up at about 10:30 in the morning, and pulled on my pants. Stretching, I walked down the hall, through the large living room, and into the kitchen-dining room, pulled along by the smell of the coffee Marsha made each morning. She sat on a floor pillow at our foot-high table, nursing her baby. She looked very beautiful, and her smile showed that she knew it in a very peaceful way. I poured myself some coffee, refilled her cup, and paced around the room, chatting with her, looking out the kitchen window at a pair of deer eating ivy on the hillside, and lighting my second cigarette of the day. Peter was in the shower, Jerry was asleep, seemingly, and Grace had left early in the morning to do God knows what; she never slept in, always rising early, especially when hung-over, and usually making up for the lost sleep with a nap in the afternoon.

"You think Grace is gonna go to the party?" Marsha asked, smiling mischievously.

"I don't know, usually, she doesn't do stuff like that."

"Yeh," said Marsha, "But she was talking about going, and maybe she's out now buying something to wear."

"Could be," I said, for once, not really caring. I knew there'd be lots of pretty women at this party, and it seemed like a good opportunity for me to meet one.

Being a Saturday, we had only one practice session planned for the day. Monday through Friday, we had two official practice sessions, and would often end up having another unofficial (attendance voluntary) one in the evening. On the day of a gig, and on the day after, we did not practice. Today, we were scheduled for 11:30. While I was fixing myself some boiled eggs and whole wheat toast, well buttered, Peter walked in wrapped in a towel. He petted Marsha and the baby, speaking soft, loving words to them, and sat down, asking for coffee. Marsha jumped up to get it for him. Their relationship, though loving, in many ways was master and servant.

"What time we gonna practice?" he asked, yawning.

"11:30," I said.

"Ugha," was his noncommittal reply. I think we all loved to practice, I know I did, but we never admitted it; our attitude was, `okay it's cool, but nothing to get excited about'. I got excited virtually every time we played. It always involved improvising solos, and the likelihood of advancing as individuals, and as a band. Usually, I was the first one in the music room.

We heard a familiar car in our driveway above, and a few seconds later, Grace walked by the kitchen window on her way to our front door.

"Hi," she said, walking down the hall towards the room she shared with Jerry.

I took my coffee back to my room, grabbed a towel, and headed for the shower. Ten minutes later, I stood clean in the living room watching Peter roll a few joints at Jerry's big oak desk. When the first was ready, he handed it to me to light while he rolled another for the rehearsal. We passed the joint back and forth, and listened to the Ravi Shankar record playing on the stereo system we all shared. I think the turntable was Peter's, and the amp and speakers, Jerry's. The music seemed intensely beautiful. I particularly loved the sound of the low strings which sounded in the bass register; they seemed ancient, and pure and serene, suggesting timelessness.

At the appointed hour, Peter and I sort of stumbled down the hall, and began tuning up. We tuned to a held-note on the little organ, having no tuner, electronic or otherwise. A short time later, Jerry and Grace walked in; Grace playing the organ, and Jerry, the drums, they had no need to tune.

Our habit at this time was to play a full set with no interruption. If we wanted to change or work on a song, we saved that for later in the day. We had learned that it was important to play an hour or so of music to develop chops and feeling, and working on a song could involve long periods of time with little or no playing, but lots of discussion!

We started on this day with "Sally Goes Round the Roses". On this song, we all had very specific parts during the singing portions of the song. This was a "cover" version of a beautiful single originally produced by Abner Specter. Years later, I met him at Chess Records in Chicago, and we each raved about how much we loved each other's versions. Ours was very unlike his; our version was kind of raga-rock. Grace sang quick, articulate ornaments that I loved then, and still do. I never saw her practice these ornaments in any organized way, but she could really do them! In the Airplane, she would sing far fewer of these. She always took the first solo in this song on the organ, and then I played. By design, we each played in very different scales, which heightened the exotic feel of the song, because Indian scales are often composed of mixed major and minor notes.

Our practice proceeded well. That is, everyone seemed to enjoy playing, we played playfully, and we didn't interrupt ourselves with arguments. The most likely to argue were Jerry and Peter. They both had very strong, and very different personalities. Jerry liked clock punctuality, and Peter preferred a looser flow; Peter was inclined to take a very long time to get ready to work, and once he was working, he had far more endurance than most. This day, no arguments.

We finished at about one, turned off the amps and the old guitar-amp P.A. we were using, and filed out of the music room somewhat dazed, as always, by the dope, the volume level, and the music itself; our ears rang. Nonetheless, we were all looking forward to the party, and we immediately went to our respective areas to clean up. Face washing, teeth brushing, hair combing, clothes changing, make-up for Grace and Marsh'.

Peter, Marsha and the kids went with me in my '54 Chevy, and Jerry and Grace drove alone. Grace had bought a new pair of jeans for the party, skin tight. With her little white cotton tee shirt, and her eyes made up dark black, almost like they do in India, she looked great.

Peter had rolled many joints, and in our car we smoked pretty much non-stop. I also drank from a half quart can of Rainer Ale while I drove, keeping it low when a cop was near, but not really worrying about anything. I had more or less chugged a first half quart at home while combing my hair, and I was starting to change from a sort of nervous, accountant on speed, which was my "normal" state, into the role I was playing; the stoned, hippie rock and roller.

If you have driven in Marin recently, and I could take you back in time to that beautiful early summer day in 1966, the first thing you'd ask would be, "where are all the cars?" and second, "where are all the houses?" For those of us lucky enough to be there, it was our own private paradise: very underpopulated, very underhoused. We were starting to complain about the traffic, but with eyes that saw the future; there was no traffic.

Curving through the green-grass hills, we got lost once, found our way again, and knew we were getting close when we started to see the cars; some were home-painted with various colors and patterns, some were old, some were new, but very never-washed dirty. Almost all in some way said, "not straight." We could see people streaming in and out, mostly in, around the side of the large house into the huge back yard with its barbecue and pool, very California. But spread across this suburban canvas were the Tribes, the Gypsies, the Earth Mothers and kids, the lawyers gone crazy, the Angels of Hell, the sweet young virgins, and recent virgins of both sexes with their healthy, long hair and budding-rose cheeks, the fat and the thin, the young and the slightly old (Neal Cassady was here. He was about forty, and I thought he was old!), the entire Fellini-scene living-art of our corner of humanity. We were so egocentric, that when we got loaded and looked at ocean waves, we said that the waves were stoned. When we looked at ourselves, we thought that the whole world was the same as we were, or rapidly becoming that way. I wonder what a pool-side party in Selma, Alabama was like on that same Saturday in 1966. Did naked men feel the rhythm of the bongos they played through their genitals, while burning ashes from the joints they held in their lips fell onto their chests, causing them to add chaotic accents to their looping, echoing drum patterns? Did they dine on hash brownies, and toast each other with L.S.D. punch? Did they swim their beautiful bodies through the blue pool waters, and the lemon-hot afternoon airs? We did!

We were arranged around the pool in enclaves, families, mini-villages, like flowers in a garden, or swarms of bees with lots of movement between groups, and cooling trips to the pool. In deference, I think, to the many vegetarians, we roasted no flesh on the barbecue, in fact we didn't cook, but ate breads and salads of lettuce, potatoes and beans. The music came from acoustic guitars, wooden flutes, and hand drums, all played by "the people", not the band members. They played singly, or in small groups, making a cacophony that was somehow, maybe it was the drugs, pleasant. There was lots of hugging and kissing, but no real public sex. Many of the women wore panties or bikini bottoms in and around the pool. During these same years, I asked a few about this practice, and they insisted that it was not modesty, but that the female genitals were ugly. Astounding!

At one point, I saw Jerry Garcia leaning against the barbecue, apparently lost in thought. John Cipollina walked up behind him, and stood looking at him, smiling. Perhaps he was thinking up some childish trick, like pouring ice on Garcia's bare back, or perhaps he was just loving his good friend. John's smile could be quite enigmatic. Jerry seemed to become aware of John's presence, and he slowly turned around, and just as slowly, a smile spread up his face that matched John's. It seemed like a long time to me that they stood there smiling at each other, kids, shamans of the music quest, elders of some mutant race. Finally, John ran sideways at the pool, and threw himself Bellushi-like into the air above the water, to land in the pool on his side, limbs askew. Garcia's smile grew first more mischievous, then philosophical, and then disappeared. He seemed to sense dark clouds on the horizon, whether in his own soul, or in the world, I couldn't know.

As soon as John was in the pool, he was joined by Peter Albin, and about ten young women. John drew people. His easy charm, ironic humor, and good looks never seemed to fail him.

Peter's head popped out of the water under which he had been swimming, and he said, "This is pretty cool!" looking widely around, and gesturing with up-turned palms.

"Yeh," said John smiling, "you want to throw Garcia in this water?"

"Sure," said Peter.

"Okay," said John, "you get a few guys and meet me back here."

"Cool," said Peter, walking away through the waist-deep water.

John was already talking to the naked young girl-woman who was standing close to him in the warm water, and by the time Peter returned, they had disappeared into the house.

"Fuck it," said Peter, not one whit disappointed.

As in one of Elwood P. Dowd's favorite phrases, the afternoon wore on. My brother Jerry and Grace didn't stay very long. Grace really couldn't seem to stand parties; it was either black-out and rage, or split. Also, for most, if not all of us, performing was so exhilarating that the rest of life was becoming just that: the rest of life. I can think of no adequate way to describe the energy of intense adulation from an audience. We bathed ourselves in the vibe, "you are wonderful." This was especially heady because, at our cores, I know we all felt inadequate and flawed.

At last, there were only ten or fifteen of us left in the back yard in the still, hot twilight.

Neal Cassady was there, his handsome face showing the ravages of his double (quadruple?) speed life, and he, seemingly drunk, raved! No "sentence" contained less than five disparate ideas, and he made no more effort at rational sense than the most obfuscating poet. To listen to him was to be roller-coastered through a fun house, every room of which was built by a different demon. There was no time to adjust to one jarring juxtaposition before the next was presented. Neal was surrounded by beautiful, very young (high school?) girls. His pull was incredible, a sort of psychic black-hole.

I stood at the edge and listened in amazement: It was like listening to someone talk improvised poetry, so fast and strong that it almost literally hurt my brain. The only kaleidoscopic mind and motor mouth I knew who could possible keep up with Neal, belonged to Ray Andersen. Recently Ray told me that Neal had visited him around this time. Ray's rather glib comment to me, "we talked."

Peter and Marsha woke up their young son, and we left slowly, Neal's words still ricochetting around us, as we walked around the side of the house.

I was stoned and drunk and happy and disappointed that I hadn't gotten laid, nor was there any prospect of sex, and tired, as I drove us back to our band house, but, about one thing I needn't have worried. The next day, my old girlfriend Leslie came to see me with only one thing on her mind, and we went up on the hilltop on a blanket in the noonday sun and fucked for all we were worth.

Last Days of Society

May came, and with it more than flowers. Peter and I were in San Francisco visiting our mutual friend Oscar, the light show guitarist. In great excitement, Oscar put an astonishing record on his turntable.

"Hey man, you've got hear this record." He started laughing and shaking his head up and down with his eyes opened wide.

It was Indian music (North Indian Classical Music), but sounded entirely different than the sitar of Ravi Shankar. This was my first encounter with the sarode, a twenty five stringed instrument, four strings of which are devoted to melody playing. These four strings are strung just above a flattened metal fretless fingerboard. The instrument has tremendous sustain, so it is possible to slide between the notes, connecting the dots as it were, in a style somewhat similar to bottleneck guitar. This was also my first encounter with India's foremost musician, Ali Akbar Khan. His absolute control of pitch, which included incredibly complex sliding ornaments, completely floored me. I could not have been more amazed. The three of us laughed repeatedly in disbelief. A ballerina with no need to return to the floor after a leap, would have been of a similar order of reality. I had never heard music of such virtuosity, and it was far from empty technique! The artist expressed the whole range of human feeling, directly touching my heart. Peter was similarly moved.

When Oscar told us that Ali Akbar Khan was coming to Berkeley to teach early morning classes, we all decided at once to enroll. There would be no interference with any band duties, and we were already employing elements of Indian music, both rhythms and scales, in our music, so this opportunity to learn more was irresistible.

Peter and I drove from Marin to Berkeley five mornings a week in my new station wagon. I always smoked a joint or two on the way, and arrived completely stoned. I had built up high tolerances, however, and I don't think my state was obvious.

As we drove along, Peter stared out of the passenger-side window at the bay and spoke lazily; "Man, just holding on to these instruments is hard!"

"No shit! The sarode keeps squirting out of my hands."

"Yeh, well I've got to balance the sitar on the bottom of my (up-turned) foot! I think it's going to take years just to get comfortable holding the thing."

"Hey man, that's one reason I decided to learn sarode instead of sitar. I couldn't stand the way you have to hold it. Besides, the fingering on the sarode's a lot more like a guitar. That thing you guys have to do of running up and down on one string to play single-note lines is just fucking crazy, man."

"Yeh, but you've got to play the sarode notes with your fingernails!...... And how long do you think it's going to take you to learn to play them in tune?"

I glanced over at Peter and back to the street as we pulled up into a parking place outside of the building where the school was being held.

"Yesterday afternoon, I started to get so I could at least play the lowest octave okay, and about half of the middle one. I don't know about the notes further up the neck, but I sure as fuck hope they'll get easier as time goes on.

"What about your finger nails?"

"They're okay now, but man, I think it's going to get very painful when they're worn down to the quick!" We got out of the car and walked in to the school.

There were approximately twenty five people in the class, of all ages, sexes, types, even two nuns in black habits with white hood-hats. Instruments were provided for our use at school, we couldn't take them home, and the class was evenly divided between sitars and sarodes.

Every morning, Ali Akbar Khan would tune all of the twenty five strings on each of the twenty five instruments while we sat silently. This took about an hour. The tuning bored some people, but to me it was fascinating and instructive, and I paid complete attention. These instruments are designed to be very sensitive. Because of a natural law of physics, when two strings are tuned to the same note, striking one will cause the other to ring sympathetically. In addition, each string produces a whole series of overtones (other notes). When the instrument is properly tuned to a particular *rag*, striking one string can cause all of the other twenty four strings to sound: reflections within reflections, as in an incredibly complex array of mirrors. ("*Rag*" or, the plural form "*raga*", means much more than scale; it designates which notes are used ascending and descending, how one moves through the notes, exactly what their pitches are, the nature and placements of their vibratos, which notes are emphasized and de-emphasized, and more.)

Ali Akbar Khan then taught us music for an hour or so. He would play a melody a few times, honing it down to something like our level, and then invite us to play it with him. We would try valiantly, sounding like any high school band in India might. Lastly, we would write it down utilizing a notation system which he was teaching us. He, and we, referred to each note by its thousands of years old Sanskrit name. He also taught us by singing and having us sing; it is an integral part of his belief system that all musicians must be able to sing what they play. In one sense this music was simple; it was archetypal. The same melody could be played by a master, and would, in that case, be enlivened by ornamentation and nuance.

To try to get us to understand the music, he would tell us stories of every sort. He might use anything from his experience to help us understand. What we call the "tonic" note, he called "Your home". He would say things like, "You can go anywhere, but you must take care how you get there, and you must remember how to get back home, and you don't want to stay away too long, or stumble getting back in. You must go home in some nice way." Oscar, Peter and I were captivated by this music, embodied as it was in Ali Akbar Khan, whom I regarded, and still do, as the world's greatest musician. His knowledge of melody and rhythm are beyond anyone's that I have heard. When asked about this, he says that his father, Allaudin Khan, forced him to practice sixteen hours a day for twenty years. Ravi Shankar came and studied with them when he was a young man; this was where he learned his music.

I had already satisfied myself that musical freedom can come only through knowledge and discipline, and Ali Akbar Khan offered himself as the path of musical knowledge. All I had to provide was the discipline to learn and to practice for twelve hours a day or so, and I knew then that, with drugs to help me, I could do it. Ali Akbar Khan never advocated drug use, in fact, he often spoke against it, but I was unwilling to take direction from him in that area of my life.

Peter and I started to talk openly around the band house about going to India to study. I thought I wanted to live the rest of my life there. I had a mental picture of saints meditating under Bodhi trees, and the tales I heard of bustling poverty and disease didn't penetrate. Indian music, which I regarded as the peak of musical evolution in the world, interested Jerry and Grace only as a source from which to take things, as in the case of music concrete. I had come to steal,
but it had stolen me.

Tom Donahue's little empire was crumbling. His partner, Bobby Mitchell, was dying, and Tom was getting heavily into drugs and becoming part of the actual scene, not an outside exploiter of it. The main problem was that, as a small label, it was hard to get the distributors to pay him what they owed. He had pressed up a few copies of our single, but they were not really distributed. We asked out of our contract, and after a few lawyer-letters back and forth, we were released. Tom's record label died, but he had another little trick up his sleeve; he became the instigator of one of the biggest communications revolutions in history: he founded underground radio.

We signed up with an L.A. manager named Howard Wolf, a delicately featured trim dynamic man who sought a record deal for us. Our contract with Tom Donahue had kept us tied up at a time when our peer bands were all being signed. We kept talking about how shitty it was not to have a contract, and Howard kept saying, "I'm working on it, big things are happening, be patient." This issue seemed to hang over our heads forever (a few months). The Airplane's female vocalist, Signe Anderson, had married and become pregnant. She and her husband were leaving to go live a more pastoral life in Oregon.

Jerry and Grace had invited Oscar to jam with us a few times, and finally, with Peter's and my approval, they invited him to play with us at our next big show. I thought it was odd that they were so casually open to Oscar, it didn't seem like their usual way, but I accepted it.

The big show was September 11, 1966. We were on the bill with the Airplane and the Dead, and we were the headliners. We had received top billing before, but never with both the Airplane and the Dead on the same show. Bill Graham was putting on a benefit for the jazz club named the Both\And.

It was crazy. It was always crazy, but this time so much more so. Costumes on top of costumes, drugs on top of drugs, you expected to see a live dancing bear in the crowd, and there was one, or a human posing as one. Ballerinas with beards, a young man turned priest of the Greek Orthodoxy for the night, Cleopatras, hookers, renaissance folks, ersatz Indians of both continents, flesh and old cloth, sequins and sweat, on and on, never stopping, occasional, brief elements repeating, but essentially changing constantly. The Fillmore had become a cement mixer.

Never had it been allowed to become so crowded. The pirates were jammed into the penitents, and Jesus could not properly parade. There was no slightest sign of trouble, oh maybe a few hearts were broken, maybe someone snapped and never returned to what we call reality, I mean there were no fights. The people seemed intensely happy and desirous of partying madly.

I think the Airplane played first, then the Dead. We waited in the musician's room, tuning up and laughing among ourselves. There were more than the ususal number of non-musicians "backstage" that night, and the presence of outsiders always caused us to knot more tightly together (remember that we weren't actually behind the stage, but above and to the side of it where we could see both the performers and the crowd). If anything was unusual with our band, other than adding Oscar into the mix, I didn't feel it. Grace spent most of the time elsewhere: in the bathroom, presumedly.

Around midnight, it was our turn. The crowd was already bananas, and man they were ready for us. Every little nuance got response, and we seemed unable do anything wrong. It felt like the audience was worshiping us, and we played with more emotion than ever before. Oscar fit right in, laying out when he didn't know the song, playing his ass off when it was his turn to solo. We crescendoed to a close with Grace screaming, "Feed your Head!" Certainly, this show has remained one of the performance highlights of my life.

When it was over, while we were packing up, my brother called Peter and me aside. He told us that the Airplane had asked Grace to join them, and that he had advised her to accept, and that she had, in fact, accepted. We had done our last show. I felt completely betrayed, and I would hang on to this sense of betrayal for approximately twenty years. How could she quit? Never mind that Peter and I had talked of quitting to go to India, she was just another showbiz asshole, me me me, fame and riches, and fuck everybody else. It is amazing to me now, how completely I was able to shift the "blame" onto her, and for how much time.

Peter and I quickly formulated a plan; we would sell our equipment, including my car, and travel to India to study with Ali Akbar Khan, essentially, forever. We invited Oscar, and he immediately accepted.

I got very drunk that night and in the morning, the hangover magnified my depression tremendously. The universe seemed to be made of shit, but "bravely" we began our preparations by calling the newspaper to place ads for our amps, guitars and cars in the classifieds.

That same day, when the mail arrived, there was in it a thick, ten by fourteen inch mailer from Howard Wolf containing a record contract from Warner Bros, the Dead's label. The contract gave us everything we could have wanted. It was too late. Our paths were chosen, we would walk them.

My bitterness was not unlike that of a jilted lover. The Airplane had not been my favorite band, so there was also an element of, 'You left me to sleep with *him*?'

We continued our preparations for India, selling things, getting passports, inoculations, and visas (a few). We had decided to go to Vera Cruz, at the tip of Mexico, and try to get work on freighters heading for India, or, at least, to book cheap passage. Oscar would travel with his wife and small daughter, Peter with his wife and two kids, I, alone. We would try to stick together.

Around the begining of October, we got on a bus for San Diego, crossed over to Tiajuana, and there boarded a train for Guaymas. We had left our drugs behind us, or rather, had used them up. I felt nervously free to be away from drugs, though soon I found that I continued to have a desire to get high (on almost anything).

The train ride was only marred by the fact that one of the toilets stopped-up, and waste spread quickly down the isle of the car, and was never cleaned up while I was there to see, though we did cover the mess with newspapers.

The train stopped frequently, and people came up to the windows to sell tamales and other delicious foods. I bought one of almost everything; it was my first taste of Mexico, and I loved it. Some items were more delicious than others, but nothing made me sick.

We slept on the beach in Guaymas, and met other young, international travelers. I had brought my first-ever guitar with me, my grandfather's, and I played raga inspired melodies on it. People seemed to take pleasure in hearing the music.

Our second night, I stayed at the beach with the wives and kids while Peter and Oscar went into town to buy food. I was sitting under a palm tree playing my guitar when one of our new friends, an Australian named Johnathan, rushed up to me.

"I've just seen your traveling companions being taken into the city jail by the police!" He was out of breath and his eyes were tall with alarm.

"Jesus Christ!........I better get in there and try to help them!"

"What you'd all better do is stay put," said Johnathan, "you"ll only end up busted yourself. At least give it some time to see if your friends can manage their own release."

A few hours later, Peter and Oscar walked up and told us they had been busted for "possesion of hypodermic needles." This developed to be a common shakedown tactic of the local police, who, at that time, were essentially licensed robbers. Money had quickly freed my friends.

We left the next day for Vera Cruz, traveling by bus, and stopping over in Guadalajara, where we went to the huge market, and Mexico (City), where we went to the anthropology museum.

We arrived in Vera Cruz, and it was a wondrous jewel. They had banned neon signs, and had kept a flavor of civilized, unhurried elegance. Poverty there didn't seem to include starvation or homelessness. Food and lodging were very cheap for us; we took rooms on the roof of a beautiful hotel. The hotel featured a three or four story, interior garden. Our rooms must have once been servant's quarters and they served us well. We met a fine-arts painter, and bought from him local, jungle-grown marijuana which was almost as strong as L.S.D., and was laughably cheap.

Our first morning in town, we were walking around looking for something good to eat when we saw an orange juice stand. Because of the difference between the dollar and the peso, it seemed to us that they were almost giving the juice away, and we all bought some. Next, we bought some pastries, also very cheap, in a little shop. We were quite naive politicaly at the time, despite our quasi-revolutionary stance, and we saw little more in the low prices than, "Wow, we can afford to eat!" The orange juice was so sweet that it was delicious with the delicate, powder-sugared pastries.

The streets were made of cobblestones, and the city was quaint, but not in a touristy way. On Saturday evening, a brass band played on the cathedral balcony above the town square while people sat on benches or promenaded peacefully, dressed in cheap or expensive, clean clothes.

It developed that there were many, perhaps thirty to fifty, people in town trying to book passages similar to those we wanted. We decided to give it a week, and then make other arrangements.

Oscar, Peter, and I, walked down to the waterfront area where the freighters tied up. The mid-morning sun was very hot, and the air smelled of tropical ocean with a touch of diesel. We had left the women and children at the hotel. The first ship we saw was the *Isolde*. Her gang plank was out, so we walked up, and Peter shouted, "Hello!" as we poked our heads through the open doorway. At once, a middle-aged man in clean, but paint-spotted work clothes walked though an interior door and looked at us inquiringly.

"Do you, SPEAK ENGLISH?" I asked, enunciating with exageration.

"A little," he replied, "can I be of service?"

"Yes, thanks. Where are you headed next?"

"Bremmerhafen."

"Would it be possible for us to work our way there, or even to book passage if you don't need more crew?" I asked, hopefully. "You must speak to the captain. I will take you to him."

He lead us through the ship, and into the presence of the captain who was friendly enough, but couldn't accomodate us. Over the course of a week, we visited all of the freighters in town and talked with the crews, but got nowhere.

We would settle on plan B; we knew that Icelandic Airlines flew from New York to Luxembourg for $170, so we would travel back up through Mexico, turn right at about Oklahoma City, go to New York, fly to Europe, and travel on, by ancient routes, to India. We knew that we would need to hitchhike a lot, so we decided to split into three groups. Mine was the smallest: me.

Desiring to make my money stretch as far as possible, I began to hitchhike north. My longest ride was with a truck driven by a kindly young Mexican man. He did not get drunk, ask for money, attempt to have sex with me, or talk non-stop, as do so many people who pick up hitchhikers. I liked him. Periodically, he would be stopped by local police who demanded, hands on guns, money to let the truck pass. As in Guymas, they had a license to steal.

I crossed into the United States at Laredo, and immediately was picked up for hitchhiking. I made up a story about my car being stolen in Mexico, and the Texas cops, mumbling about "those fucking Mexicans," gave me a ride out of town. I continued to hitchhike, and arrived in Oklahoma City exhausted.

Suddenly, the prospect of hitchhiking on with no rest was just more than I could face; I decided to spring for a Greyhound ride to New York. The bus was absolute luxury to me: regular bathroom and restaurant stops, a warm clean seat on which to sleep. It was heaven.

In New York, I went directly to the airport, bought a ticket on Icelandic, ate, slept a few hours on a bench in the airport, and boarded the plane for Luxembourg. My guitar had gradually broken apart in Mexico, so I had given it to a small poor child who was delighted to receive it. I had one cloth satchel, and a U.S. Army-issue sleeping bag of World War II vintage. I was about to travel overland to India.

Dream...

New York is in the lower, middle. A white, stone promenade begins at New York, and curves, like a crescent moon, first left, and then to the middle again. To the right of the path, is ocean, to the left, nothingness. I walk to India which is located at the top of this curving walkway, having many adventures along the way. Sometimes, I go by boat and have boat-related adventures. The dream recurs regularly for twenty five years and counting. The episodes change in each dream, but the set is always the same, like some huge board game. India is always a Himalayan village where students work at music.

12

The Hippies Get Their Hit

I arrived in Luxembourg, again, or still, exhausted. I took a room in a small clean old pension, and planned to awaken early to catch a train going southeast into and through Germany, but I overslept, so I needed to stay another night. That second night, I hardly slept at all, I was so rested up and excited about actually beginning my Journey to the East. Early the following morning, I boarded a train and rode straight to Stuttgart. There, I got on the Orient Express for Istanbul.

This was not the modern, refurbished luxury train that it has become. It was more akin to the spy novel version, and carried people of all economic circumstances, but was most laden with Turkish laborers returning from stints in Germany. Many people brought their own food, as the fare in the dining car was relatively expensive and not very good. I slept in my seat, although for periods of an hour or so, I sometimes found benches on which to lie. During waking hours, I watched, fascinated, as the German landscape which I knew well from my teens, metamorphosed into darker, Balkan terrain. The thatched roofs became thicker, pointier and more primitive. The demeanor of the customs police in the Communist countries was at once arrogant and hostile. Sometimes they literally threw my passport back at me, while they steadied their shoulder-slung machine guns with one hand.

Then, we sped south through Greece and on to Istanbul across plains of sunshine.

I loved Istanbul at first sight. The writer Herb Caen used to be fond of calling San Francisco "Baghdad by the Bay." It would be stupid to call it "Istanbul by the Bay", but how similar San Francisco and Istanbul are: the hills, the combinations of cultures, the constant reemergence of water views. They are even both, in some sense, gateways to the East. I couldn't get enough.

Within a few days, I met a young local who for five dollars, sold me a resinous piece of hashish about the size of a large candy bar. He glanced quickly about us with a tight forced smile on his face as we made the exchange standing in front of the Cook's Tours office. My new "friend" was a short man with black hair and gleaming eyes. His caution was like that of a surf-fisherman: constant yet practical, unemotional. He spoke broken but very expressive English, and undoubtably many other languages, as well as his native Turkish. He looked to be about my age: 22. I asked him about the drug laws here.

"The law are very strict," he said, "but for yourself it is not a worry. For me (here, he jabbed himself repeatedly in the chest with his index finger) if they catching me, it's many years in jail. But perhaps my brother could help me." He offered no explanation of how his brother might be in a position to help. He seemed in no hurry to get away, and we talked for some time, about Istanbul and my trip to India, he smiling constantly and with laughing, impish eyes. I didn't doubt that he did things to survive that I might not approve of, but who was I to judge him? I liked this man who called himself "Joe" to me. I wonder what he would have called himself if I had been Japanese? I didn't bother to ask how to re-contact him, because the block of hash I had bought from him was bigger than I could imagine using here, and I had no willingness to carry drugs across borders.

Not wanting to smell up my hotel room with hashish smoke and risk arrest, I began to eat some. At first, I ate only a little, and got only a little stoned, but I became bolder one evening, and ate a large piece right before heading out. By the time I arrived in the brightly lit shop section of the New

City, I reeled like a drunk. I was barely able to get back to my hotel, and, as I pulled myself by the bannister up a flight of stairs, the manager stuck his head out of his office. He looked at me with a mixture of sadness and disgust.

I had come this far wearing the long hair of the hippie, but was beginning to feel that it made me too negatively conspicuous, so I went to a barber and got a rather short haircut. Next, I went to a western (as opposed to eastern which was also available) clothing store and bought a dress shirt and a necktie. These I wore with a corduroy coat and jeans which I had brought along. I still looked plenty scruffy, but more like a poor student than a hippie. Was I selling out or growing up? You decide.

I needed a visa to pass through Iran, so I went to their Istanbul embassy. I waited in a room with about ten hippies to see the responsible person. Though I had arrived last, I was called first, and inside the secluded office the Secretary said, "Did you see those others? We will make them wait many days, and then we will refuse the permission." My change of look had allowed me to proceed.

I took a train to the border of Iran, and began once more to hitchhike. I didn't stand by the road with my thumb out, but spoke to travelers at roadside settlements. So much was changing before my eyes. As I traveled east, objects which had been considered garbage, began to be of value; a Coke bottle could hold liquids, therefore it was worth saving. If someone discarded it, someone else would pick it up. In Istanbul, red chile peppers are ground and used as condiments. As I traveled eastward, the peppers became more prominent until, in India, they were sometimes the food itself.

In Tabriz, Iran, I met an Iranian student who was returning home, overland, from his studies in Germany. His name was Akmed. He was about six feet four inches tall, and looked very strong. He walked with cocky arrogance, the epitome of Middle-Eastern macho. People literally jumped out of our way as we walked along the streets together. His english was very good, and he told me of his, and the whole Muslim world's love for the great American boxer Muhammed Ali.

"At last all Muslims have a champion in the west," said Akmed, "and not just a champion in the boxing sense. Muhammed Ali is an upright, moral man. His refusal to join the army and fight for American imperialism makes him dear to all of our hearts. My fondest wish is to meet him someday."

I had mixed feelings about this stuff. When I left the States, I felt bitter about America's many problems. Already, as I traveled, I saw that governmental obtuseness seemed to be everywhere. And personal freedom, which I valued tremendously, was very great in America. I had felt that there must be many countries that were freer and more humane than the United States. Now I was not so sure. Emotionally, I felt like the person who says, "I can put down my family any way I want, but don't you try it, that's my *family*, Goddamn it!" Still, my bitterness was real.

As we continued walking, a middle-aged man dressed in poor clothing chanced to not jump out of my friend's way fast enough. Instantly, Akmed was ready to fight the man for having been slow to jump. Though the exchanges were in a language I didn't understand, I could easily tell that the man was apologising profusly; he made every physical gesture of subservience. He looked down, bowed his head, clasped his palms in front of himself, and spoke in low respectful tones. My companion evidently decided it was unnecessary to kill the man, and we walked on.

He had traveled the whole region repeatedly, and he showed me the non-tourist ropes. He took me to an inn that was frequented by caravans. In fact, a caravan was forming in the courtyard when we arrived. The inn consisted of large, empty rooms surrounding a huge, interior court. Groups of travelers would hire the rooms, bringing with them thick wool rugs on which to sleep, sit, work, cook, in short, to live. Their animals, mostly camels, would stay in the courtyard, sheltered and safe behind a guarded gate. With Akmed translating, I learned that these caravans still, in modern times, span the distance of India and China in the east, to the interior of Germany in the west. I was astounded that this way of life continued with such vigor, unimpeded by frontier guards.

I parted from my new friend in Teheran, and continued asking people for rides. Two Pakistanis who had lived and worked in England offered me a ride if I would drive, to which I readily agreed. Their tiny Opel sedan was full of German electronic equipment such as radios and tape decks, which they must have known they could sell at home for a profit (probably a large one). I drove us along happily for hours as all sign of civilization dropped away behind us. It felt good to have a steering wheel in my hands again.

Somewhere in an Iranian desert, one of the car's springs broke, and we had to spend two days in a little village getting it welded together again. Both men wanted to leave me there in the middle of nowhere, but they were terrified of driving now, because of the springs, so they allowed me to continue. Desert turned into foothills, then mountains.

The man in charge of the border guards in a high mountain pass at the edge of Pakistan, was apparently an old friend of theirs. He was an army colonel, and he fed us a wonderful meal in his military post, while, outside, the wind howled wildly. The building, and its amenities were mostly western, and we accepted his invitation to stay the night. A framed picture of one of his predecessors, a fierce looking man with long, waxed mustaches, hung in my room. The toilet, down the hall, was decidedly non-western. It was comprised of two small, rectangles on which to stand (crouch), and a tiled hole in the floor. The trick of crouching to defecate was not one which came easily to me, but at least I did not fall in.

A day or two later, we arrived at their home town, Quetta, Pakistan. Quetta was a large city, but I don't recall seeing any building of more than two stories. My friends ordered their wives to cook for us, which they did. The women placed the food in the "living room" and withdrew.

"What about your families," I asked, "aren't they hungry?"

"Don't worry about them. They always eat separately. They prefer it."

I never saw them, they were baggy shadows covered in loose cloth from head to foot, and they stayed only as long as there was a specific task to perform.

I slept comfortably and in the morning took a train for Karachi, from which I hoped to go by boat to Bombay, India. I was getting close!

In Karachi, a big port city which, though ancient, has every modern convenience, I had my first taste of American food since leaving Mill Valley. Walking through the sky-scrapered downtown section, I saw a large Chinese restaurant. I went in, recognized everything on the menu, and picked items I often order at home. Everything tasted exactly as it had tasted when I was a kid in Palo Alto, and it was as welcome to me as any hamburger has ever been to any American abroad. I have told this story to a few friends, and they have told me of having had this experience in South America and Africa, in fact, virtually everywhere. How fortunate for travelers that there is at least one universal cuisine.

No ships were leaving for Bombay that I could afford, and it would cost money to wait for a cheaper ship. Pakistan and India were having border disputes so I couldn't travel overland; my only real choice was to fly to Delhi, which I did.

In Delhi, I went by cab to the train station and bought a first class ticket (very cheap) for Calcutta. The train cut across the heart of Northern India, and through its windows I saw vibrant green vegetation growing from brick red clay, as can be seen in many tropical countries. Water buffalo lolled in muddy trenches, and, in stations, men wearing only loin cloths bathed from water spigots.

There were no westerners in the train-car in which I rode, and one Brahmin youth lorded it over the other riders, ordering them about mercilessly. For reasons which I don't understand, he did not attempt to subject me to his rule but treated me with a phony deference, allowing his contempt for me to show through clearly. Was it Walt Kelly who said, "We have met the enemy and he is us."?

I arrived in Calcutta tired, hungry, with little money, and in a confused state. The trip had taken so long, I had gone through so many changes, that I could barely remember why I had come.

I had heard that the Y.M.C.A. would be a good place to stay for a few days, so I went there by taxi. The "Y" was clean and cheap. I shared a room with a young man who had come from a village a thousand miles to the south to work in Calcutta. He spoke english in the style popularized by Peter Sellers.

"Call me Rabi," he said, "that's what my friends do."

There were, other than I, no westerners among the fifty or so men living at the "Y". Their stories were all similar; they were well educated, and sought work, and its compensations, beyond what the village could offer.

I knew that drugs and alcohol wouldn't go over here, they were expressly forbidden, so the day after I arrived, I began searching for a more comfortable location. I found it in an Indian hotel that catered to working people, most of whom were very similar to those at the "Y": bank clerks and civil servants, an army of paper pushers. I started to picture villages filled only with old people, women, and kids, as sometimes pertains when all of a country's young men have been killed in war. These men were not dead, of course, but merely exiled in relative modernity so that they could support their people. They told me that they missed their families, but felt themselves choiceless slaves, luckier than others in that they were able to work and send money home. There was a bar in the hotel, and I often drank the cheap local whiskey with these men while they told me of their homesickness. I had, even while traveling, begun to feel homesick myself.

As in Vera Cruz, my room was on the hotel's roof. The toilet was in a small, freestanding room, also on the roof; though I was the only westerner in the hotel, the plumbing was, to my relief, western.

Nearby, was the city's largest indoor bazaar, an ancient dusty and mysterious place. The starting point of the exotica was the stuffed set-piece of the mongoose and cobra locked in deadly combat; there were other odder items to be had. I wound my way through the bazaar's serpentine maze until, deep inside, I found a little shop which looked seedy enough to be promising.

"Do you speak English?" I asked.

"Yes, how can I help you?"

I looked about to make sure we were alone. This did not seem to suprise him. "Do you know where I can buy some marijuana?"

"You want the leaves of the plant?"

"Yes."

"We name that `ganja'. If you will wait a few minutes, I will get you some."

"Fine."

On this, my first visit, he sold me a very low grade of marijuana. When I came back a few days later and expressed my dissatisfaction, he asked if perhaps hashish would be more to my liking. I agreed, and soon I was preparing cigarettes in my room with hashish. I would remove the tobacco from a standard filter cigarette, mix it with hash and reinsert it, making a cigarette that looked very normal. These, I smoked while walking through parks, botanical gardens, and on lakeside paths which were within half a block of my hotel. I tried to appear casual, and changed direction frequently as I walked so as to remain downwind from others. I don't know what the laws were, but I had come to understand that most Indians, especially "upper class" educated ones, looked down on drug use.

I learned that Ali Akbar Khan was not in town, but he had told me to check in with his son, Ashish Khan, when I arrived, so after perhaps a week, I presented myself to him. He was practicing with a young drummer, and graciously invited me to stay and listen, and have tea with them. I was amazed by his virtuosity on the sarode, and delighted by his kindness to me. He told me that he would help me to get a good sarode, and within a few days, I had an excellent one.

I began to attend classes at the Ali Akbar College of Music in Calcutta, and met many students, all of whom were from India. Within a few weeks, one of them, named Azir, invited himself over to visit me in my hotel room.

"Hello," I said, as I opened the door for him, "Welcome."

"Hello," he smiled, "as you see, I have brought my sarode with me."

"Good," I said, "why don't you put it on the bed and have a seat in the chair there."

He did, and, sitting across my little table from me, he began to tell me what was on his heart.

"You have studied an entire summer with Khansahib (Ali Akbar Khan)?" he asked.

"Yes," I replied.

"You are very fortunate, and perhaps you don't realize how fortunate you are." (This was undoubtably true, and in more ways than he could have realized). "Khansahib" he continued, "only seldom teaches here now, and I myself, though I have been attending the college for almost five years, have never had the opportunity to study with him. There are people who treasure for a lifetime the one lesson that they have had with him, and already you have studied an entire summer!"

I didn't know what to say. We had all considered ourselves lucky (I can remember saying, "Its like having Beethoven here to to teach you!") but we hadn't really understood.

"Please," Azir said, "when you see him again, tell how much we want his teaching here. Try to persuade hime to give us some of his time!"

Again, I didn't know what to say. For one thing, I was not in a position to persuade Khansahib of anything. I made some weak statement to Azir, and we spoke of other things. He played a little for me and I was impressed with how in tune his notes were (I was still really struggling with intonation). We had a cup of tea and he left.

For several hours I lay on my bed in my new white Indian clothes (baggy pants and long, collar-less shirt). If Khansahib taught only infrequently here, why was *I* here? I began to intuit that Ali Akbar Khan would never really live in India again, and that he would live, instead, in California. I don't know why I thought this, he had only stayed in California for two summers while he had taught there, but I couldn't shake the thought.

Weeks became months, and I had no word of Peter and Oscar. They neither arrived, nor wrote. Christmas eve, I found myself sitting in the hotel's funky little bar. It had been decorated for Christmas in hoplessly inappropriate ways (perhaps by the same person who writes the battery insertion instructions that accompany Formosan toys). The hotel had hired a piano player to play their small upright. He was dressed in a dirty and shabby white tuxedo. He wore white gloves to match his outfit while he played, and his idea of where the notes were, seemed quite approximate. The tables were filled with lonely men trying to be happy, or at least make it through.

Perhaps two weeks later, I got a letter from my father. He told me that I was a failure who squandered money. His tone was angry, and I have no doubt that he was worried about me. Only a few days later, I got a very different letter from him. Before I had left Mill Valley, I had, with great uncaring, given the Airplane permission to do "Somebody to Love." They had done it, and it was becoming a hit: the first true, hippie hit.

Here I was in Calcutta which, by now, I hated, with no friends, and no Ali Akbar Khan; I felt a lot of self pity and resentment. I had always wanted to have a hit, so I decided to go home and enjoy it. I was so far culture shocked, that I didn't even want to return to Mill Valley. I wanted a penthouse apartment in San Francisco with wall to wall shag carpeting and a ceiling of sprayed-on paper mache with little gold sparkles. I mean, man I was sick!

On the jet home, I bought a cigarette lighter from the stewardess at an exorbitant price, and it seemed to symbolize my new state. I drank good scotch, and ate western food. I had been in Calcutta for four months and my stomach had boiled almost the whole time from various sicknesses and the white-hot food (and drink).

At the San Francisco Airport, I felt almost like kissing the ground. I went by taxi, quite expensive, to Jerry and Grace's San Francisco house. They greeted me warmly, if somewhat cautiously; they knew how angry and hurt I was about Grace's leaving the band. I did feel that way, but I also loved them and was happy to be back. We didn't speak of unpleasant things.

The Airplane was playing that night at a nightclub named the Hungry I, and they invited me to come. They were on the bill with Dizzy Gillespie, and, after the 'Plane's set, he invited them to jam with him. They accepted, and in that famous jazz tradition, he launched into a song in five/four time, pretty much leaving them in the dust. By now, I could jam along easily in five/four, and it pained me to sit and watch them flounder, and know that I could cook.

It sure didn't pain me that my song was a hit, though. I couldn't turn on the radio without hearing it, and people congratulated me wherever I went. My head began to swell along with the heads of the other, by now, successful hippies. It was of this period that Bill Graham, referring to the Airplane, said, "They think that when they walk across the street, it's ballet." Money and adulation seem to hurt each new generation of musicians, at least those lucky enough to achieve popularity.

One day, Grace called and told me that Paul Mc Cartney was in town. Did I want to come by the Fillmore during the afternoon to meet him and jam with him? I was so into myself and my drugs. "Yeh, maybe I'll drop by a little later." I said.

C. Slick

Me playing tanpura, 1969

C. Slick

Ustad Zakir Hussain, his wife Tong & me, Berkeley 1974

OUR WEDDING, MOUNTAIN VIEW 1967
all photos by B. Slick

Carol & I

Carol & I

My Mother & Grace

Me, Oscar & Grace

Jerry, me, Carol & Jean Piersol

Epilogue

I never showed up. Instead, I married a beautiful young woman named Carol, had two kids, studied with Ali Akbar Khan full time for twelve years, continued to write and play, became a very into it alcoholic and drug addict, and lost almost all of my worldly possessions. As of this writing, I am coming up on four years clean and sober. I'm in a program that helps me to maintain my sobriety and to progress spiritually. Our oldest son is in his twenties, and he plays the bass with me. Our younger son loves surfing and rap music.

As Allen Ginsberg said, "I have seen the best minds of my generation..." The toll has been awful. So many good friends, so many wonderful musicians, have died young. But sobriety is spreading. I hope those of us who survive can build upon the timeless, good values we have so painfully learned: community, love, art.

In the long process of shepherding this book from an idea to a reality a number of people gave assistance and advice for which the publishers are grateful.

First we would like to thank Stanley Mouse not only for his original painting on the cover but also for spending a very hot day in Sonoma photographing the color posters reproduced herein. To Chet Helms, Wes Wilson, Alton Kelly and Stanley Mouse for allowing us to reporduce the 4 GREAT SOCIETY posters in the color insert. Also special thanks go to William Reid for allowing us to use his GREAT SOCIETY poster as our frontispiece. To Ray Andersen of the Holy See for his photographs of the GREAT SOCIETY recording session as well as his GREAT SOCIETY posters. Don Sortor for his myriad contributions to the process as well as his willingness to listen. Thanks to Steve at Kings Baseball Cards in Berkeley for allowing us to borrow posters out of the shop. To those individuals and organizations whose assistance we failed to record, we thank you collectively.

The text of the book is set in Stone Serif. The chapter titles are set in Bodoni Poster.

ALSO AVAILABLE FROM
SNOW LION GRAPHICS / SLG BOOKS

		PRICE
MIPAM, by Lama Yongden paperback, ISBN 0-9617066-0-0		$12.95
THE UNVEILING OF LHASA, by Edmund Chandler		
	paperback, ISBN 0-9617066-1-9	$12.95
	hardback, ISBN 0-9617066-2-7	$14.95
WIND BETWEEN THE WORLDS, by Robert Ford		
	paperback, ISBN 0-9617066-8-6	$12.95
	hardback, ISBN 0-9617066-9-4	$19.95
LANDS OF THE THUNDERBOLT, by Lord Ronaldshay		
	paperback, ISBN 0-9617066-6-X	$12.95
	hardback, ISBN 0-9617066-7-8	$19.95
A TIBETAN ON TIBET, by G.A. Combe		
	paperback, ISBN 0-943389-02-X	$12.95
THE ELEGANT TASTE OF THAILAND, by Kongpan & Srisawat		
	paperback with gateway fold, ISBN 0-943389-05-4	$19.95
HEALING IMAGE: THE GREAT BLACK ONE,		
	by WIlliam Stablein, Ph.D.	
	paperback, ISBN 0-943389-06-2	$14.95

To order: Add US$1.75 postage for the first volume; 75 cents for each additional volume. California residents add 7%. Postal rates may change. Foreign postal rates are higher. All prices in US dollars. Make cheque payable to SLG BOOKS.

SLG BOOKS
P.O. Box 9465
Berkeley, CA 94709
USA

Tel: 510-841-5525
Fax: 510-841-5537

Roger Williams

Stanley Mouse, Sonoma 1991

Roger Williams

The Author, Berkeley, 1991

the great ! society

OPENS TUES
MARCH 15TH

THE MATRIX
3138 FILLMORE
NEAR LOMBARD
567-0118

THE MOST EXCITING GROUPS AND PERFORMERS APPEAR AT THE MATRIX — SAN FRANCISCO'S MOST UNIQUE NIGHTCLUB.

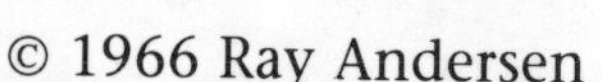